DATE DUE

DEC 0 7 2005			
NOV 2 7 2006			
GAYLORD			PRINTED IN U.S.A.

THE BEST DIVE WRECKS
OF THE WORLD

WHITE STAR
PUBLISHERS

1 Metal wreckage rising from the wreck of the Ghiannis D is home to a wide variety of organisms, surrounded by schools of fish.

2-3 This Vickers Viking sank after suffering damage in the Gulf of Mortoli, Corsica. The plane lies in water only 43 ft (13 m) deep.

4 This Taiwanese fishing-boat sank on Echuca shallows at Kavieng in Papua New Guinea.

5 top Tube sponges grow on the Superior Producer, a Dutch ship that sank in Curaçao in 1977.

5 center The Ghiannis D lies at the northwest tip of Abu Nuhas reef. It sank on 19 April 1983 during a voyage from Rijeka to Hodeida.

5 bottom A scuba diver swims among swarms of glassfish near the wreckage of the Carnatic, which sank on the Abu Nuhas Reef.

7 The prow of the Japanese destroyer the Fumizuki rises vertically in Truk Lagoon, Micronesia.

8-9 The wreck of the Dino, a decommissioned merchant ship used for target practice at the nearby Capo Teulada firing range in Porto Zafferano, Sardinia, lies about 79 ft (24 m) deep.

CONTENTS

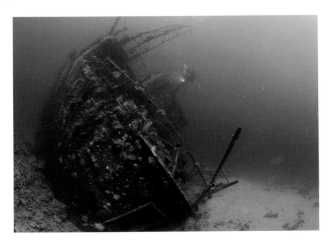

EDITED BY
Egidio Trainito

TEXTS BY
Kurt Amsler
Massimo Bicciato
Claudio Cangini
Thomas Easop
Stephen Frink
Vincenzo Paolillo
Roberto Rinaldi
Egidio Trainito
Alberto Vanzo

DRAWINGS BY
Claudio Nazzaro

GRAPHIC DESIGN BY
Maria Cucchi

TRANSLATION BY
Studio Traduzioni Vecchia, Milan

© 2003 White Star S.r.l.
Via C. Sassone, 22/24
13100 Vercelli, Italy
www.whitestar.it

ISBN 88-544-0014-9

REPRINTS:
2 3 4 5 6 07 06 05 04

Printed in China
Color separation by Chiaroscuro, Turin

INTRODUCTION

BY EGIDIO TRAINITO

*"There is no experience more chilling
than swimming through a shipwreck . . ."*

CLIVE CUSSLER

The most ancient vestige of a ship is a reindeer antler, worked in a surprisingly sophisticated manner, that was used to build the framework of a boat which was probably covered with hides. It dates back to 10,000 years ago and comes from Husum on the North Sea, in the Schleswig-Holstein region of Germany. But there are few doubts that humans traveled seas, lakes and rivers before that, by simply gripping onto tree trunks or straddling them and paddling with their arms, as the Aborigines of Australia still do today.

Today, millions of boats navigate our planet's lakes and rivers. Primordial pirogues like those commonly used in Madagascar or Sulawesi, coexist with enormous cruise ships, immense aircraft carriers and the most modern sailboats, can be navigated by just one person, and are capable of once unthinkable speeds. The story of how man learned to travel by water is also told by an immense underwater gallery of boats, ships, and a whole array of items that have allowed humans to travel, trade, fight and work on the oceans. There are civilian and warplanes, land vehicles, trucks, tanks, batteries of cannons, oil platforms, and cranes. Probably few of the countless devilries invented by man are not underwater somewhere.

There is an impressive number of these underwater museums. Underwater archaeologists calculate, with a small margin of error, that there is a shipwreck every quarter mile/500 meters along the more than 5000 mi/8000 km of Italy's coastline — and this conservative estimate includes only shallow waters. The situation seems comparable on the high seas: four ancient, almost completely intact ships were found during a search for the wreck of the DC9 that crashed about 10,000 ft/3000 m deep in Ustica in 1980. And Robert D. Ballard's recent prospecting in an American nuclear submarine has revealed at least 8 wrecks in a small area near Banco di Skerki, in the central southwestern Mediterranean. This is not only true in the Mediterranean, where the history of navigation is old and traces the paths of the greatest ancient civilizations, including the Egyptian, Phoenician, Greek, and Roman. In fact, North America's Great Lakes, which cover a surface area a little over 85,000 sq. miles/220,000 square km (small compared to the 140 million sq. miles/360 million square km of oceans) have recorded almost 50,000 shipwrecks. These start with the explorer Sieur de la Salle's **Griffin**, swallowed by the waves in 1679. The coast between Florida and Maine is an uninterrupted ship cemetery, and even the waters of the Mississippi hold more than a thousand sailing ships and steamships that once carried people and cargo.

The almost uninterrupted succession of wars that have been fought on every sea of the planet has provided vital additions to this immense underwater museum. From the age of Homer (whose Iliad tells us that the Achaeans used an armada of 1156 ships in the expedition against Troy) to the present, wars fought at sea have led to the sinking of thousands upon thousands of ships, as well as every other marine weapon of war. In World War I alone, the US Navy lost 100 ships and the US Merchant Marine lost 200; and in World War II 1216 mercantile ships flying the US flag were sunk.

Wars, storms, structural failures, navigational errors and human error of every type have always been the cause of shipwrecks. In most cases, these wrecks have become accessible only over the past 50 years or so, with the development of increasingly sophisticated technologies that allow man or human-controlled machines to explore the ocean depths. So the great discoveries of underwater archaeology are still quite recent, as are the enterprises that have helped bring the great tragedies of the sea, like the **Titanic** lying 4000 meters below the waves, back before our eyes. Similarly, in every part of the planet, from the Great Lakes of America to the vast Pacific, the adventurous spirit of a growing number of enthusiasts is repaid as they visit the thousands of wrecks that a simple air tank makes accessible to them.

This book discusses the most beautiful shipwrecks in this small part of our underwater museum. There are no famous ships here, like the **Andrea Doria** or the **Titanic**, which are either too difficult to reach or too deep, nor will you find the vessels used to develop the science of underwater archaeology. But you can enjoy a virtual underwater exploration of every corner of the planet through all the shipwrecks that can be explored with just a bit of scuba diving experience.

There is a magical moment when you dive down to a wreck: you descend deeper and deeper into the blue sea, and only the noise of bubbles breaks the silence. You suddenly see the outline of the ship and can begin to decipher its fragments. This is the thrill you'll experience.

And you can also relive the history of the wreck. The experience becomes magical as you strive to uncover the past, lifting the veil of memory often lost in time. The story is always tragic, even when there was no loss of human life. When a ship goes down, the person who owned her, commanded her and often loved her is always hurt — not only by the economic damage, but above all because the feelings, aspirations, dreams and sometimes entire lives of many men and women were bound to that ship. These are the stories you'll hear.

" THERE IS A PORT OF NO RETURN, WHERE SHIPS
MAY RIDE AT ANCHOR FOR A LITTLE SPACE
AND THEN, SOME STARLESS NIGHT THE CABLE SLIPS,
LEAVING AN EDDY AT THE MOORING PLACE...
GULLS, VEER NO LONGER. SAILOR, REST YOUR OAR.
NO TANGLED WRECKAGE WILL BE WASHED ASHORE.

LESLIE NELSON JENNINGS   "LOST HARBOR"

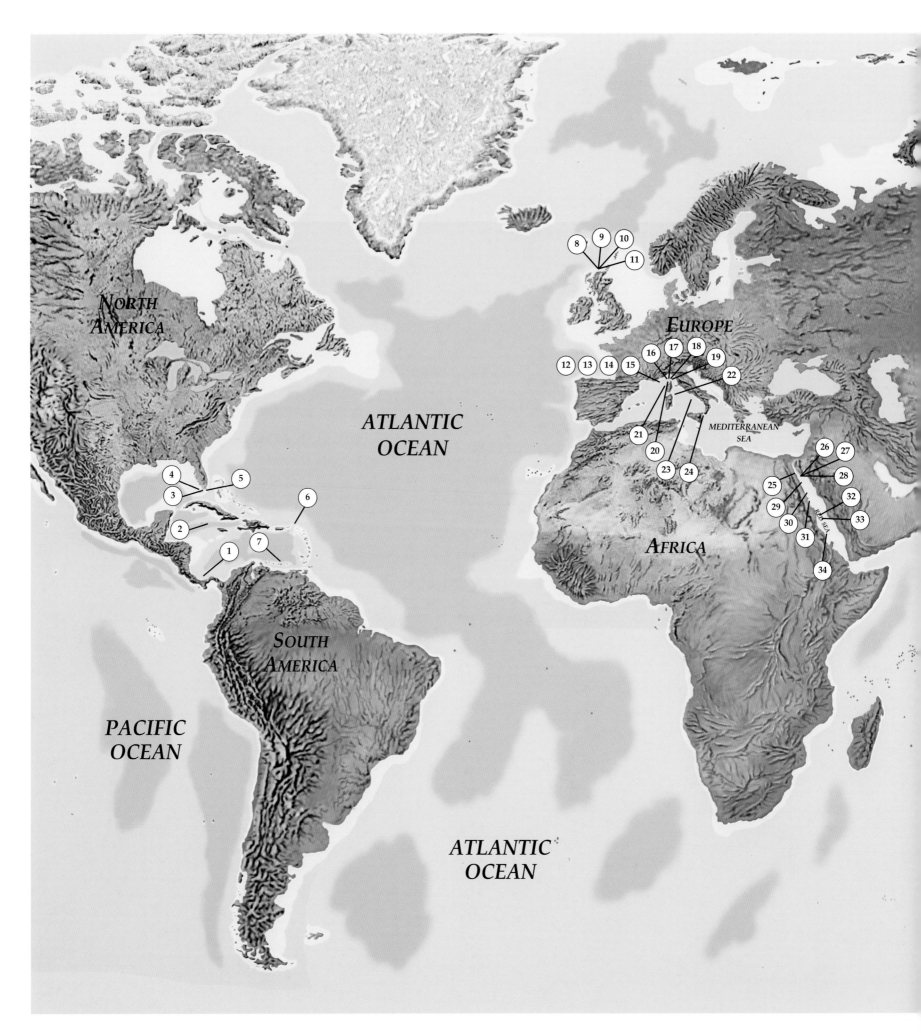

NORTH
AMERICA

EUROPE

ATLANTIC
OCEAN

MEDITERRANEAN
SEA

AFRICA

SOUTH
AMERICA

PACIFIC
OCEAN

ATLANTIC
OCEAN

RED SEA

ATLANTIC OCEAN
1) JADO TRADER
2) RUSSIAN DESTROYER
3) EAGLE
4) BIBB
5) SPIEGEL GROVE
6) RMS RHONE
7) ANTILLA
8) HMS ROYAL OAK
9) SMS BRUMMER
10) SMS CÖLN
11) SMS KRONPRINZ WILHELM

MEDITERRANEAN SEA
12) LIBAN
13) MESSERSCHMITT 109
14) PROSPERO SCHIAFFINO
15) RUBIS
16) HAVEN
17) GENOVA
18) SESTRI KT
19) SESTRI ARMED CARGO SHIP
20) B-17 E
21) VICKERS VIKING
22) KT 12
23) LST
24) LAURA C

RED SEA
AND INDIAN OCEAN
25) THISTLEGORM
26) GHIANNIS D
27) CARNATIC
28) CHRISOULA K.
29) NUMIDIA
30) TUGBOAT
31) CARGO SHIP
32) BLUE BELT
33) UMBRIA
34) NAZARIO SAURO
35) "SHIPYARD"

PACIFIC OCEAN
36) SHINKOKU MARU
37) AIKOKU MARU
38) SAN FRANCISCO MARU
39) FUJIKAWA MARU
40) SANKISAN MARU
41) MITSUBISHI F1 M2
42) MITSUBISHI A6 M2
43) TOA MARU
44) GRUMMAN F6 F3
45) B-17 E
46) SS YONGALA

ATLANTIC

BY EGIDIO TRAINITO

T he Phoenicians had already pushed out to the coast of Portugal, where they built their staples, and Viking ships were the first to reach the coast of North America. But it was the voyage of Columbus that opened the route to the west and began transforming the Atlantic into the busiest ocean in the world.

We all know what the consequences were, but we may not be aware that over time, the coasts of Central America and the islands of the Caribbean have become one of the most extraordinary ship graveyards in the world. Indeed, it is no accident that this is where the legends of sunken treasure first arose. Galleons loaded with gold and silver and fabulous vanished treasures have sparked the imaginations of entire generations, becoming the ruin of many adventurers and the fortune of few. In the Caribbean Sea, a small island in the Lesser Antilles, Barbuda, has for almost 200 years based much of its economy on salvaging flotsam and jetsam from ships that founder on its reefs, backed by authorization from the British government (The Right of Wreck). Caribbean wrecks are very popular with tourists, and there are hundreds of dives that allow enthusiasts to experience the thrill of discovering them and learning about their history. Diving conditions make Caribbean wrecks even more attractive: with few exceptions, wrecks in the Caribbean Sea are in warm, clear water at depths that make them accessible to divers with almost any level of experience. Most of the wrecks lie on white sand seabeds that provide excellent illumination. And many Caribbean wrecks, like the *RMS Rhone*, a steam sailing ship that has

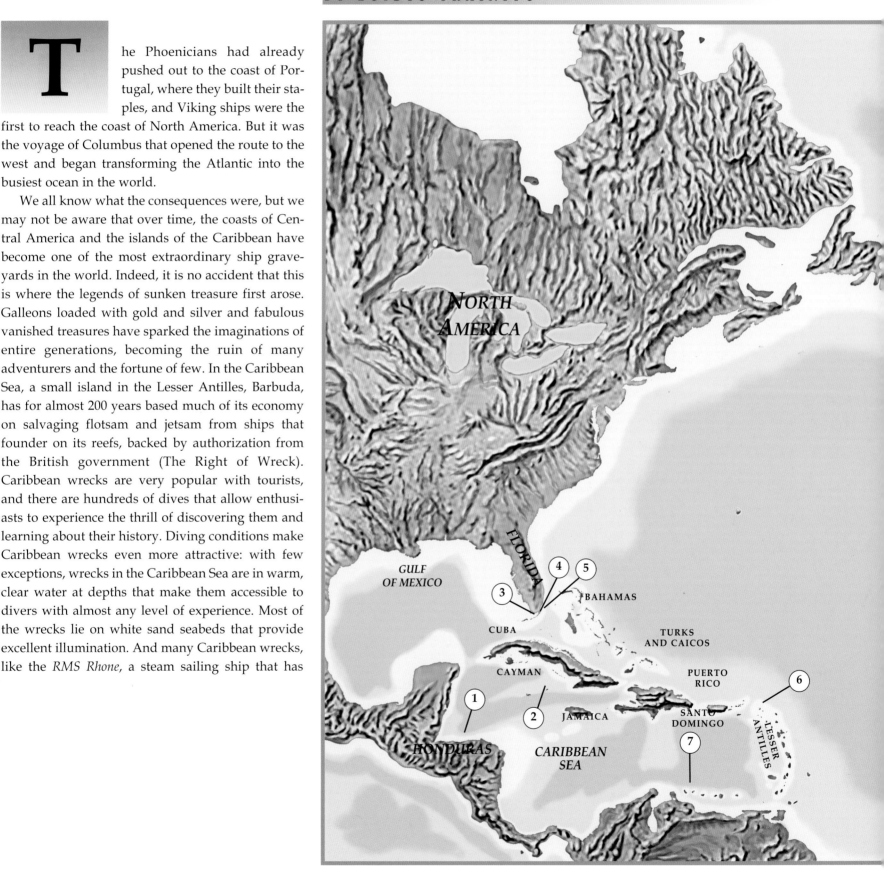

OCEAN

ORKNEY ISLANDS

8
9
10
11

IRELAND

GREAT BRITAIN

FRANCE

SPAIN

ATLANTIC OCEAN

AZORES

CANARY ISLANDS

AFRICA

CAPE VERDE ISLANDS

N

1) Jado Trader

2) Russian Destroyer

3) Eagle

4) Bibb

5) Spiegel Grove

6) RMS Rhone

7) Antilla

8) HMS Royal Oak

9) SMS Brummer

10) SMS Cöln

11) SMS Kronprinz Wilhelm

ATLANTIC OCEAN

been lying off the British Virgin Islands since 1867, are full of history. Many others have been sunk to create new diving areas and further stimulate the adventurous spirit of scuba diving enthusiasts. In the Florida Keys, Aruba, the Cayman Islands and many other places, transport ships, warships and airplanes that have been abandoned and restored have helped increase the already extraordinary endowments of this Caribbean underwater museum, and some of them have been described in the pages of this book. Even in Bermuda, where divers can explore a total of 53 wrecks, almost all in easily accessible shallow waters, the *Hermes*, lying on a seabed 82ft (25 m) deep, was intentionally sunk in 1984 by the Bermuda Divers Association.

While few of the wrecks in the Caribbean are related to wars, the end of World War I was what caused most of the events at Scapa Flow in the Orkney Islands on the other side of the Atlantic. The wrecks of Scapa Flow, to which many of the pages in this book are dedicated, are just a few of the ships that made up the entire German war fleet — 70 ships including battleships, cruisers, and destroyers — which were interned to guarantee the armistice and scuttled in 1919. Although not all of them can visited and many have been salvaged over the years, the wrecks of Scapa Flow are a major destination for scuba enthusiasts. Diving conditions are quite different from the Caribbean: in Scapa Flow, the temperature is always cold, fluctuating between 6° and 12° C (43° to 54°F), with visibility only 30 ft (10m) even under the best of circumstances and depths that often exceed 100 ft (30m). Strong tides also create powerful currents that make it necessary to descend and ascend along your moorings. So, while the Caribbean is for everyone, the wrecks of Scapa Flow offer dives for expert divers with appropriate equipment.

14 A yellowtail snapper parades before the wreck of the Jado Trader, *the shrouds still drawn tight around her protruding mast, offering an ideal substratum where a myriad of organisms can prosper.*

15 In Bermuda, a scuba diver swims on the wreck of the Montana, *a steamship with paddle wheel propulsion. The large wheel that moved the blades is still in perfect condition, as the photo shows.*

JADO TRADER

BY ROBERTO RINALDI

Here we are in the waters off Guanaja, ready to dive onto the wreck of a small mercantile ship, the *Jado Trader*. This ship was sunk for the pleasure of scuba divers in order to create a point of interest and a refuge for the repopulation of fish and corals. Yet the story of the *Jado Trader* contains a few mysteries and thrills, making a visit to the shipwreck a bit more interesting. The little vessel transported fruit from the islands to the continental ports of the Caribbean Sea.

But one day, an inspection by Honduras police revealed the presence of a load of drugs. Mangoes and bananas covered illegal drug trafficking that had probably gone on for years among Caribbean ports. After

this last voyage, the *Jado Trader* was confiscated and remained docked at the port. She slowly fell into disrepair, and it was not until the mid-1980s that a group of travel operators decided to buy her and sink her for the specific purpose of creating an artificial reef and an alternative to the other beautiful dives on the coral reefs of the island. After they received the appropriate authorizations, it was an easy task to drag the little vessel out a few miles to a protected area of sandy sea floor near two lovely coral pinnacles rising 112 ft (34 m) from the flat seabed to about 50 ft (15 m) from the surface. Today the *Jado Trader* is still there among the corals, resting on its starboard side on the sandy floor. It's unfortunate that she's's lying on her side, as a shipwreck is always more

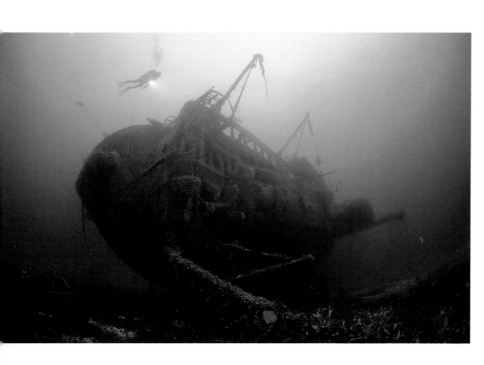

16 top The Jado Trader *lies on her starboard side: note the capstans on the deck, still in good condition.*

16 bottom The after section of the Jado Trader *is the most interesting to visit, although the bow is spectacular when you descend from the reef right in front of it.*

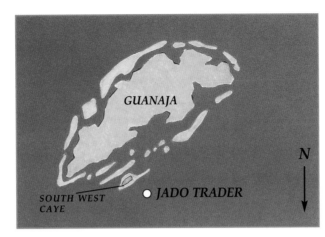

GUANAJA

SOUTH WEST CAYE

○ JADO TRADER

N

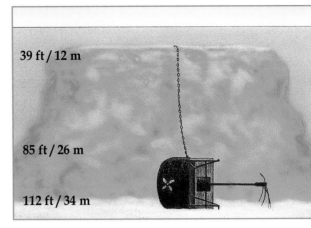

39 ft / 12 m

85 ft / 26 m

112 ft / 34 m

TECHNICAL CARD

TYPE OF WRECK	Cargo ship
NATIONALITY	Unknown
YEAR OF CONSTRUCTION	Unknown
DATE SUNK	1985
CAUSE OF SINKING	Creation of a reef
LOCATION	South-east of South West Caye, Guanaja, Honduras
DISTANCE FROM SHORE	2 miles / 3.5 Km
MINIMUM DEPTH	85 ft / 26 m
MAXIMUM DEPTH	112 ft / 34 m
LENGTH	230 ft / 70 m

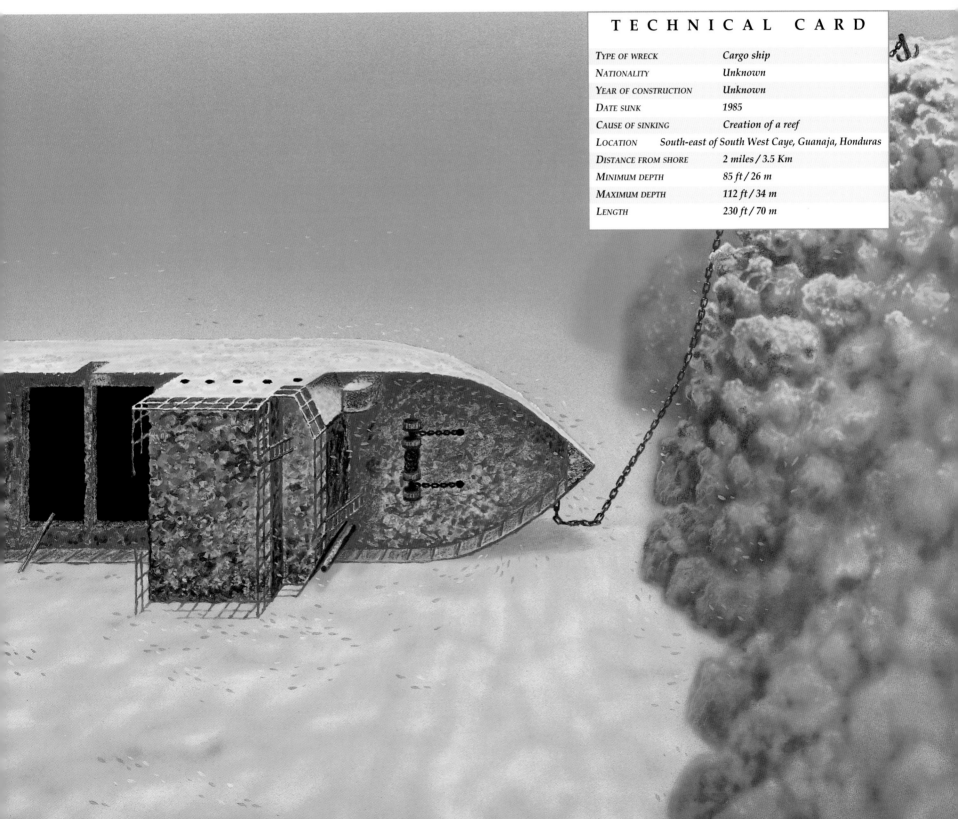

interesting when it has come to rest in an upright position. The chains on the anchors that were lowered into the sea to guide her sinking are still visible. The little ship rises about 85 ft (26 m) from the seabed, where you can see the port side bulwark, the part closest to the surface. The bow is pointed to one of the two coral pinnacles, to which the mooring line of the diving center's boats is tied. Just descend a little way along the mooring line to admire the beautiful coral wall in its entirety and get a glimpse of the outline of the wreck standing out against the bright sandy floor. The first sight of the bow is very

JADO TRADER

18-19 Because of the transparent water, it's not difficult to get an overall view of the entire ship.

18 bottom left This is the view of the ship you'll see when you descend from the slopes of the reef, to which the mooring rope is secured.

18 bottom right A grouper has chosen the safe structures of the wreck of the Jado Trader *as its home.*

19 top A large, menacing moray protrudes from its den.

19 center In addition to encrusting sponges, many branching sponges have also begun to develop, reaching truly spectacular sizes.

19 bottom The bow capstans are magnificently colonized by large numbers of colorful sponges.

evocative and spectacular in the blue water, with its upper portion covered with tufted gorgonians. This beautiful sight is heightened by the presence of a couple of large groupers; accustomed to divers, they will probably escort you to the wreck. On the fore deck, the capstans are encrusted with red sponges and inhabited by a large number of coral fish. Look carefully: right above the upper capstan near the port side bulwark is a cleaning station where parrotfish and small groupers gather. There is nothing else of interest on the fore deck, which you can pass quickly, swimming toward the small forecastle.

Your next stop is the entries to the hold and bunks. Impressive masses of tiny silver fish live there, thousands of them all together, ready to flee in an instant like the shards of an explosion. Two gigantic green morays live in this part of the ship. They really are enormous! They swim quickly and elegantly, coming boldly up to meet you. But don't be intimidated: they're simply creatures who are accustomed to meeting divers, often taking food from their hands, and have no hostile intentions. From here, you can glimpse the second coral pinnacle in the distance, although your attention will

continue to be drawn to the structures of the interesting stern, which has the largest colonies of sponges, corals and other encrustations and the most reef fish.

The fish you'll see include great blue parrotfish and spectacular angelfish. The ship in herself does not offer much, except for a gas stove and a bathroom, reminders of the days when sailors lived on board.

At this point, all that remains is to descend to get a look at the propeller and return to your route, swimming along the upper bulwark, now abundantly colonized by gorgonians.

RUSSIAN DESTROYER

BY STEPHEN FRINK

Sunk as a dive site on September 17, 1996, this ex-Russian destroyer is one of the most dramatically placed wrecks in the world.

The vessel is perched on the edge of Cayman Brac's north wall, pointing out into the blue depths. Silhouetted against the bright morning sun, the high, sharp bow looks like a huge raised sword as you swim beneath it at 110 ft (34 m). Up on the foredeck at 60 ft (19 m), the twin barrels of the 76.2-mm cannons on the bow remind you that this was once a proud warship. A similar gun mount is also intact on the after deck. The ship was built in 1984 in Nakhodka, Russia, as a missile frigate and carried the official designation number 356, which is still plainly visible on the side of the hull.

The ship is 330 ft (100 m) in length and has a beam of 43 ft (13 m). Her relatively light weight of 1,590

metric tons was achieved by using steel for the hull and aluminum for the superstructure. Twin 8,000-hp diesel engines were fitted for normal maneuvering, with twin 10,000-hp turbines capable of driving the ship at speeds in excess of 30 knots for high-speed pursuit.

The ship was acquired from the government of Cuba and prepared for sinking by the Cayman Islands Department of the Environment, the Cayman Watersports Association, the Sister Islands Tourism Association and local volunteers. She was renamed *M.V. Captain Keith Tibbetts*

20 top left and bottom This destroyer, now decommissioned, was sunk on September 17, 1996 to create a scuba diving attraction.

20 top right The ship, 312 ft (95 m) long and 43 ft (13 m) wide, was built in Russia in 1984 as a missile-launching frigate.

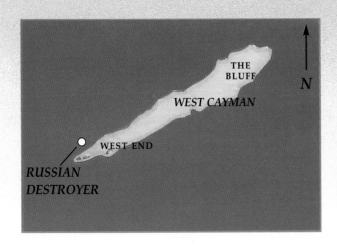

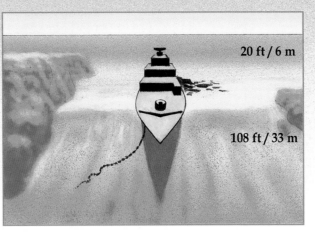

20 ft / 6 m

108 ft / 33 m

TECHNICAL CARD

TYPE OF WRECK	Destroyer
NATIONALITY	Russian
YEAR OF CONSTRUCTION	1984
DATE SUNK	September 17, 1996
CAUSE OF SINKING	Creation of a reef
LOCATION	Off the coast of Cayman Brac, Cayman Islands
DISTANCE FROM SHORE	50 miles / 80 Km
MINIMUM DEPTH	20 ft / 6 m
MAXIMUM DEPTH	108 ft / 33 m
LENGTH	328 ft / 100 m

in honor of one of Cayman's pioneers in the dive industry, however dive operators may refer to the wreck alternatively as the "Keith Tibbetts," the "356," or simply the "Destroyer." The scuttling was accomplished by pumping water into the ship, leaving the wreck completely intact at the time of sinking.

Two moorings are attached directly to the ship, one on the stern and one on the bow. Divers normally head directly for the bow since this is the deepest part of the dive. The depth beneath the keel at the bow is about 80 ft (24 m), with the sand falling away to about 110 ft (34 m) directly under the tip of the bow. The forward section of the main deck is at 50 ft (15 m) and the stern deck is at 45 ft (14 m). The bottom under the stern has been gradually filling with sand, but is generally around 60 ft (18 m). Visibility on the wreck is normally around 100 ft (31 m), although winds from the north may stir the sand up a bit.

The ship is easily penetrated in a number of places, in part owing to deterioration of the superstructure from storm surge and electrolysis. During the winter of 1997-98, a large section of the center superstructure collapsed during a storm and fell to the port side, exposing entry points

RUSSIAN DESTROYER

22-23 The spectral bow of the Russian destroyer known as the Keith Tibbets faces the side of Cayman Brac.

22 bottom left Even when seen from a distance, the massive after section of the Russian destroyer stands out clearly.

22 bottom right The after section of the destroyer is interesting owing to its impressive antiaircraft artillery.

23 top Entering the Russian destroyer is a difficult enterprise, but you can swim over it.

23 bottom left A dolphin that has become the divers' mascot frequents the waters where the Russian destroyer lies.

23 bottom right The wheel-house of the Russian destroyer is in good condition and shouldn't be missed.

previously sealed off. The aluminum structures above main deck level continue to deteriorate at a faster rate than the steel hull.

Care should be taken in entering newly accessible areas as new openings appear, since there are many potential snags. Wreck-diving experience and equipment may be required to safely penetrate some areas.

Although the clarity of the water and relatively shallow depth makes the ship seem immense at first, there is no need to rush the dive. Most divers find there is ample time to make at least one complete circuit of the ship, pausing to enter the bridge and several other interior areas.

The guns naturally draw a lot of interest, but the most fish life can be found around the intricate radar mount. Only about 30 ft (9 m) below the surface, this is the shallowest part of the ship.

Larger animals, including green morays, hawksbill turtles, Nassau grouper and jewfish, have taken up residence on the wreck over the years. Spotted eagle rays and an occasional giant manta also seem to include the wreck in the home territories.

EAGLE

BY STEPHEN FRINK

Overgrown with encrusting corals and sponges and home to thousands of reef fish, the *Eagle* one of the favorite wreck dives in the Florida Keys.

She lies on her starboard side in 110 ft (34 m) of water off the coast of Islamorada, sunk there on December 19, 1985 by members of the Islamorada community and the Eagle Tire Company.

Originally named *Raila Dan*, this vessel was later named *Barok, Carmela, Ytai Carigulf Pioneer, Aaron K.* and finally *Eagle*. Constructed in Werf-Gorinchem, Holland, in 1962, the *Eagle* was 269 ft (41 m) long with a beam of 40 ft (12 m).

Powered by a 10-cylinder diesel engine, she was capable of cruising at 12 knots. During the later portion of the ship's life, operating as the *Aaron K.*, the *Eagle* was used to transport paper and cardboard from the U.S. to Central and South America. On October 6, 1985 fire broke out in the machinery spaces while en route from Miami to Venezuela, damaging the vessel beyond repair and destroying much of the superstructure.

After being towed back to Miami, the *Aaron K.* was cleaned and

24 top The Eagle *began her career as a cargo ship shuttling among the islands, and ended it as scrap moored on the Miami River. Through subsidies from the Eagle Tire Company and the hard work and investments of local scuba divers, she has now become a very popular diving site.*

24 bottom In a fine display of pyrotechnics, the Eagle *was sunk on December 19, 1985, and has now become an artificial reef.*

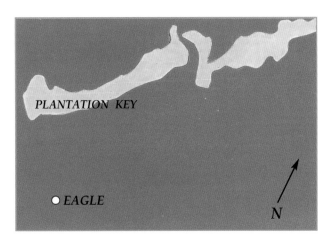

PLANTATION KEY

● EAGLE

N

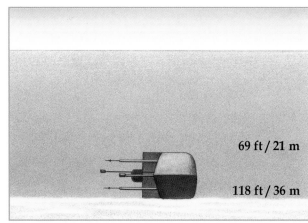

69 ft / 21 m

118 ft / 36 m

TECHNICAL CARD

TYPE OF WRECK	*Cargo ship*
NATIONALITY	*Dutch*
YEAR OF CONSTRUCTION	*1962*
DATE SUNK	*December 19, 1985*
CAUSE OF SINKING	*Creation of a reef*
LOCATION	*Off the coast of Islamorada, Florida*
DISTANCE FROM SHORE	*5 miles / 8 km*
MINIMUM DEPTH	*69 ft / 21 m*
MAXIMUM DEPTH	*118 ft / 36 m*
LENGTH	*285 ft / 87 m*

prepped for diver safety and one final voyage was taken to the waters off Islamorada.

Explosives planted by the Metro-Dade Bomb Squad were used to sink the vessel.

Simultaneously, a series of harmless but spectacular charges were set off along the superstructure to add to the excitement of the event. Unfortunately, there was a problem with the way the ship was ballasted, and she settled onto her starboard side, covering up large holes that had been carefully cut for diver entry and exit. However, the combination of open hatches and explosion holes leave numerous entry points for divers. Caution should be exercised prior to penetration and a guide is recommended.

The exterior of the ship has many areas of interest, including the completely encrusted crow's nest on the after mast. Sticking straight out from the ship at around 95 ft (29 m), the crow's nest is surrounded by large schools of fish.

At about the same depth on the opposite side of the wreck is the large

26 top Heary encrustation has covered the Eagle. *Compare this photo of the top with the one taken in 1985, opposite page.*

26 bottom left The propeller, imposing and richly covered with colorful sponges, is a true delight for divers.

prop and rudder, also well covered with coral and sponges. A pair of cargo booms on the after section of the ship add more habitat for marine life. Forward of the crow's nest there is a large open hatch that runs the entire width of the ship. The main mast and a smaller forward mast jut out into the open water like the crow's nest of the after mast, attracting clouds of fish.

The *Eagle* is located about five nautical miles off of Islamorada, three miles northeast of the Alligator Reef light. Depths on this dive range from 69 ft (21 m) to 118 ft (36 m).

Visibility is normally 32 ft (10 m) to 65 ft (20 m), with greater visibility frequently encountered when the position of the Gulf Stream is favor-

EAGLE

26 bottom right
It is not possible
to enter the deepest
recesses of the
Eagle, but divers
can visit the holds.

27 top right
The hold of the
Eagle now is home
to dense schools of
little grunts, and
sometimes giant
groupers.

26-27 The Eagle,
shown here in a
1985 photograph,
first came to rest on
her starboard side,
but was later
cracked in two by
powerful breakers
swollen in 1998 by
Hurricane George.

27 bottom Ever
since the Eagle was
sunk, the top has
been popular with
underwater
photographers.

able. Currents change from day to
day and may be very strong. These
currents are generated by the Gulf
Stream or eddies from the Gulf
Stream, rather than by tides, so there
is no way to predict them in advance.

In 1998, the *Eagle* was broken in
two by Hurricane George, opening
up a substantial gap between the two
halves of the hull. The propeller,
which formerly hung clear of the bottom, is now partially buried in the
sand and the crow's nest is about 15
ft (5 m) shallower than before. The
relatively clean break created instant
access to additional areas below the
main deck, but penetration should
only be attempted by trained and
experienced divers.

BIBB

BY STEPHEN FRINK

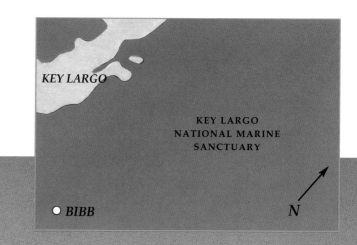

KEY LARGO

KEY LARGO
NATIONAL MARINE
SANCTUARY

● BIBB

N

TECHNICAL CARD

TYPE OF WRECK	Coastguard Cutter
NATIONALITY	US
YEAR OF CONSTRUCTION	1936
DATE SUNK	November 27, 1987
CAUSE OF SINKING	Creation of a reef
LOCATION	South of Molasses Reef, Key Largo, Florida
DISTANCE FROM SHORE	6 miles / 10 Km
MINIMUM DEPTH	95 ft / 29 m
MAXIMUM DEPTH	131 ft / 40 m
LENGTH	328 ft / 100 m

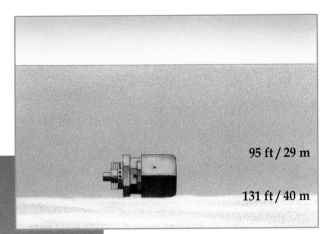

95 ft / 29 m

131 ft / 40 m

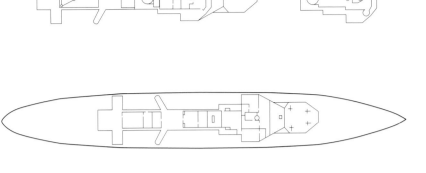

29 top The drawing shown alongside features a reconstruction of: above, details of the superstructure of the bridge (complete in the central part); below, the plan of the first foredeck. Built in 1935, the Bibb was almost a hundred meters long and 12,5 meters wide; with its two Westinghouse turbines and streamlined form, it could reach a speed of twenty knots.

T he *Bibb* is a former U.S. Coast Guard cutter named for Secretary of the Treasury George M. Bibb. Built in 1935, she was 327 ft (100 m) long with a 41-ft (12-m) beam. Powered by twin Westinghouse steam turbine engines that developed a total of 6,200-hp, she had a maximum speed of nearly 20 knots.

Her armament consisted of one five-inch gun mounted on the fore deck and four 50-caliber machine guns. Her crew included 12 officers and 116 enlisted men.

The ship was sunk in 1987 by a coalition of local businesses, south of Molasses Reef and just outside the former boundary of the Key Largo National Marine Sanctuary. When the larger Florida Keys National Marine Sanctuary was established in 1991, additional protection was provided for the wreck.

The *Bibb* sits on her starboard side in 130 ft (40 m), with the shallowest portion of the hull at about 90 ft (27 m) and the bottom at 130 ft (40 m). The superstructure of the ship above

29 center The crow's nest of the American coastguard vessel Bibb is adorned by luxurious formations of coelenterates and deep-sea gorgonians.

29 bottom The Bibb is now home to a large quantity of sponges, hydroids, hard and soft corals; the nutritious substances carried by the currents, at times fast, sustains abundant growth.

the main deck was prepared for divers, but owing to the sideways orientation, penetration can be difficult and should only be undertaken by divers with the proper training, experience, and equipment.

Fifteen years on the bottom have given the ship a thick and colorful patina of encrusted marine life. Deepwater sea fans, sponges and hard corals grow in clumps on every suitable surface, providing excellent habitat and food for thousands of reef fish and invertebrates.

The *Bibb* served in the North Atlantic during most of World War II, where her 12,000-mile range kept her busy escorting convey vessels back and forth across the Atlantic. During one crossing she rescued 202 sailors from the torpedoed troopship *Henry Mallory* and 33 sailors from the freighter *Kalliopi*. In 1945 she was transferred to the Pacific where she helped establish an advanced operations base near Okinawa. The late 1960s saw her back at war again, this

30 left The Bibb *lies on her right side, at a depth of about 131 ft (40 m).*

30 top right The impressive size of the Bibb's *propeller will reward the diver.*

31 top left The photo reveals the great charm of the marine creatures living around the Bibb.

31 top right Stephen Frink, portrayed framed by sponges and corals, while he photographs the Bibb.

time in Vietnam as part of operations Market Time and Sea Lords. The Bibb also has an historical tie to the Florida Keys. Another Coast Survey vessel named *Bibb* was sent to the Keys in 1851. That voyage was the first scientific study of the coral reefs in the Florida Keys, led by Swiss biologist Louis Agassiz.

The *Bibb* is located about six nautical miles offshore, in an area that is frequently blessed with clear, blue water spilling over from the edge of the Gulfstream. Visibility is normally 50 ft (15 m)to 100 ft (30 m). The good visibility often comes with a strong current, which varies frequently and may even change during the course of a dive.

31 center The Bibb, in an image taken from the bow, is a coastguard vessel with the characteristic long, and streamlined shape.

31 bottom left A photographer takes a picturesque photo of the bridge of the Bibb.

SPIEGEL GROVE

BY STEPHEN FRINK

32 top *The* Spiegel Grove *had launched in 1955. The ship vaunted a wide, well-shaped bridge, designed to transport amphibious vehicles for attacks.*

32 bottom *The vessel was sunk on 17 June 2002, 5 miles (8 Km) off the coast of Key Largo, in Florida.*

The *Spiegel Grove* is a behemoth among wrecks, the largest vessel ever made into an artificial reef for divers at the time of her sinking on June 9, 2002. An ex-naval amphibious assault ship designated LSD-32 (Landing Ship Dock), the *Spiegel Grove* is 510 ft (155 m) long and has a beam of nearly 82 ft (25 m). Even resting on her starboard side in 131 ft (40 m) of water, the ship comes to within 95 ft (29 m) of the surface. The wreck is located about five miles offshore from Key Largo, Florida, in the Key Largo National Marine Sanctuary.

The *Spiegel Grove* was launched by Ingalls Shipbuidling Corp. of Pascagoula, Mississippi, on November 10, 1955. The ship's unique design is built around the commodious well deck, where a variety of amphibious assault vehicles can be carried. A complex system of internal tanks allowed up to 17 feet of water to flood the well deck, creating a sea-going dock. The entire stern could be opened or closed by a massive, hydraulically operated gate, permitting up to 21 mechanized amphibious craft to drive in and out with ease.

About a third of the well deck was spanned by an enormous helicopter deck, which could be used for as many as eight helicopters, or for storage space for trucks. Two high-capacity cranes allowed the *Spiegel Grove* to load and unload its cargo of vehicles without outside assistance. The long arm of the starboard crane broke free of its mount when the ship sank, and extends out over the sand. The boarding ladder that was used to evacuate the ship when she sank prematurely is still attached to the hull, next to the port crane.

The *Spiegel Grove* depended primarily on other warships and aircraft for protection, but three twin anti-aircraft guns provided a measure of defense. One gun mount is

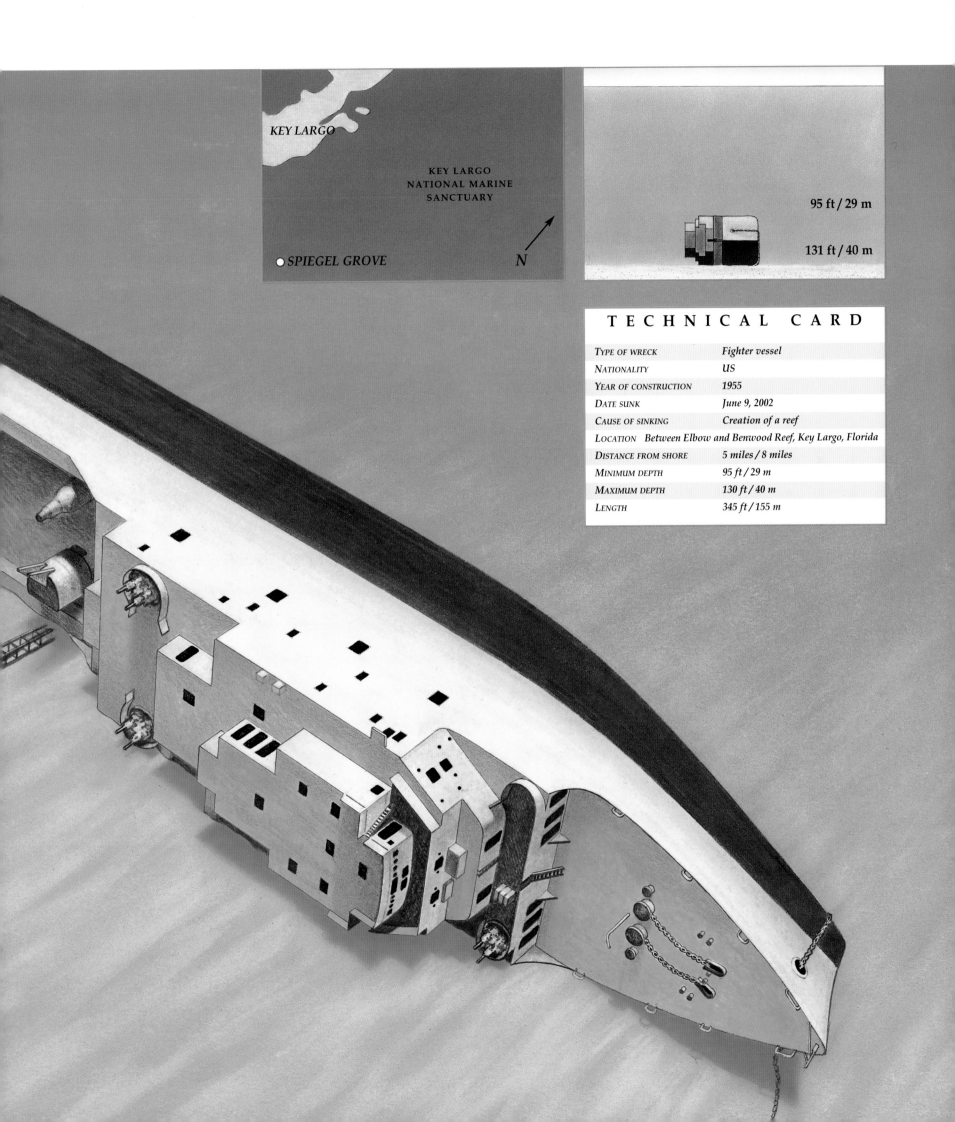

KEY LARGO

KEY LARGO
NATIONAL MARINE
SANCTUARY

○ SPIEGEL GROVE

N

95 ft / 29 m

131 ft / 40 m

TECHNICAL CARD

TYPE OF WRECK	*Fighter vessel*
NATIONALITY	*US*
YEAR OF CONSTRUCTION	*1955*
DATE SUNK	*June 9, 2002*
CAUSE OF SINKING	*Creation of a reef*
LOCATION	*Between Elbow and Benwood Reef, Key Largo, Florida*
DISTANCE FROM SHORE	*5 miles / 8 miles*
MINIMUM DEPTH	*95 ft / 29 m*
MAXIMUM DEPTH	*130 ft / 40 m*
LENGTH	*345 ft / 155 m*

on the starboard side forward of the superstructure, and the other two are port and starboard aft of the superstructure. The barrels were cut off when the ship was decommissioned, but otherwise the gun mounts are largely intact and can be easily recognized by their prominent recoil springs.

The uppermost deck of the ship is the 03 level, also known as the navigation deck. The wheelhouse is located here and a bronze plaque describing the history of the ship can be found on the after bulkhead, at about 95 ft (29 m). In the Command Information Center, directly behind the wheelhouse, several radars are still mounted, along with an old analog tracking table. The captain's day cabin is located on the starboard side, and various offices occupied the remainder of the deck.

The next deck down, the 02 level, is nearly twice as large as the navigation deck and contains the wardroom and staterooms for officers of the ship, landing craft, aircraft and marines. The 01 level is the most largest and most complicated of the upper decks. In addition to berthing spaces for the ship's crew, this deck is where the mess hall and

SPIEGEL GROVE

The name *Spiegel Grove* comes from the Ohio estate of Rutherford B. Hayes, 19th President of the United States. During her commissioned service from 1955 to 1989, the ship conducted two humanitarian tours of Africa, distributing food, clothing and medicine, and served with the Sixth Fleet off the east coast of the United States and in the Mediterranean.

In addition to the removal of contaminants and general clean-up performed prior to sinking the ship, several provisions were made to improve diver access and safety. First, all the doors above the main deck were either removed or secured in the open position. Second, 4-foot by 4-foot holes were systematically cut in the bulkheads and decks above the main deck to provide "up or out" escape routes. Third, a series of guide lines were installed on each deck above the main deck. Except for the line which runs through the galley on deck 01, all of the guide lines begin and end at openings to the ocean.

A system of red and green mesh markers was also installed on each line. Going in the direction of the green mesh will provide the shortest way out, although since the ship landed sideways, this may not necessarily be the shallowest route.

Six moorings were installed after the ship was on the bottom, arranged along the port side from bow to stern. Use of the moorings is free, but due to high demand the normal etiquette is to vacate your mooring after one dive rather than sit on it during your surface interval.

Diving conditions can be highly variable at the site, but a substantial current is often present. Depending on wind strength and direction, wave action may also be high. Visibility averages around 50 ft (15 m), but can be anywhere from 20 ft (6 m) to 120 ft (37 m).

34-35 The Spiegel Grove *is more than 82 ft (25 m) wide; even if it lies on the side at a depth of no less than 131 ft (40 m), the ship therefore arrives to 95 ft (29 m) from the surface.*

34 bottom The winches may be found on the first level of the foredeck.

35 top The two enormous five-blade propellers provided 23,000 horsepowers.

35 bottom Before she was sunk the Spiegel Grove *was modified to guarantee she would be safe for divers, and plans were implemented to make her more accessible.*

galley are located. The "Spiegel Beagle," a cartoon Snoopy riding an alligator, can be found on the deck in the thwartships passageway on this level, about 95 ft (29 m) deep.

The main deck, or 00 level, is partially split by the forward end of the well deck. Exiting the superstructure at the forward end of this level will lead you out to the foredeck, where the anchor windlasses are located. Toward the stern, this level exits to the main deck along the top of the well-deck wing walls. Berthing space for the ship's complement of 300 marines can be found on this deck.

Most points of interest are on the superstructure side of the ship, but several features make it worth visiting on the hull side on at least one dive. The two huge five-bladed propellers are here, along with the shafts and rudders. Driven by two steam turbines putting out a total of 23,000 shaft horsepower. These propellers could cruise the Spiegel Grove at 21 knots. If you want a photo of yourself with the name of the ship in the background, you can find it in two places at the stern. One is on the side of the hull, the other is on the back of the stern gate.

RMS RHONE

BY STEPHEN FRINK

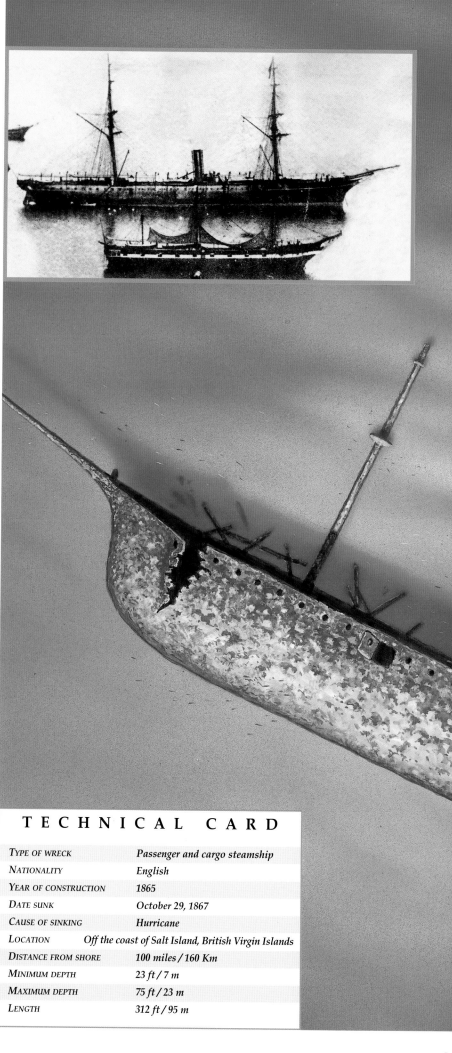

T he tragic sinking of the Royal Mail Ship *Rhone* in 1867 was a catastrophe that still reverberates faintly within the steel hull of the ship. A total of 173 lives were lost when the ship broke in two on Black Rock off Salt Island in the British Virgin Islands. Fewer than 30 survivors were rescued, including one who spent the night clinging to the foremast.

The *Rhone* was a new design launched in 1865 for the Royal Mail Steam Packet Company, the first commercial vessel to use a shaft-driven propeller. She was primarily steam powered, but carried a full set of sails as well. Lean and rakish looking with an overall length of 310 ft (95 m), the *Rhone* was fitted with a number of luxurious cabins in addition to her cargo compartments.

The events that resulted in her eventual loss began with an outbreak of yellow fever in St. Thomas, which required the ship to anchor in Great Harbour Bay off Peter Island to take on coal and provisions before continuing her voyage to South America. An exceptionally strong hurricane struck violently during the night of October 29, 1867, causing the *Rhone's* anchor to drag even while Captain Wooley applied full power. When the eye of the storm passed over, the decision was made to run for the open sea, where the captain believed the ship could safely ride out any storm. The anchor, though, was now jammed hopelessly on the bottom. After considerable delay trying to raise it, the captain cast off the chain and steamed away. Skirting a known shallow area around Blonde Rock, the *Rhone* tried to slip through the narrow pass between Salt Island and Dead Chest, but was driven hard onto the rocks and broke in two. Ironically, the anchorage at Great Harbour Bay would probably have been

TECHNICAL CARD

TYPE OF WRECK	*Passenger and cargo steamship*
NATIONALITY	*English*
YEAR OF CONSTRUCTION	*1865*
DATE SUNK	*October 29, 1867*
CAUSE OF SINKING	*Hurricane*
LOCATION	*Off the coast of Salt Island, British Virgin Islands*
DISTANCE FROM SHORE	*100 miles / 160 Km*
MINIMUM DEPTH	*23 ft / 7 m*
MAXIMUM DEPTH	*75 ft / 23 m*
LENGTH	*312 ft / 95 m*

TORTOLA

GORDA

N

RMS RHONE

23 ft / 7 m

75 ft / 23 m

36 top The Rhone, acquired in 1865 by the Royal Mail Steam Packet Company was essentially a steamer but it featured complete sails. 312 ft (95 m) long, the Rhone had both cargo holds and several luxurious cabins.

36 bottom Thanks to the particularly clear waters and a wide-angle lens, it is possible to get an idea of how enormous the Rhone is.

an excellent place to ride out the second half of the hurricane, after the wind shifted direction following passage of the eye.

The bow section is the most intact portion of the ship, lying on its starboard side in 70 ft (21 m) of water. The graceful bowsprit extends far out over the sand, encrusted with sponges and coral. The inside of the hull is almost completely coated with orange cup corals. Easy access to the interior can be found in the vicinity of the mast, which sticks out prominently over the sand supported by the crow's nest, or from the massive tear in the hull at the back of the bow section. Use caution entering the bow section, as diver contact and even exhausted air bubbles cause small but cumulative damage.

The wooden deck has rotted away, but ten of the steel beams that supported it remain. They stand upright, looking curiously like the columns on a Greek temple. Another set of seven deck beams can be found with more wreckage, further from the bow. Both sets of beams are thickly coated with brilliant red, yellow and purple sponges, making them a favorite sight for divers. The entire wreck is thick with fish, some harboring naturally within the various structures for protection, including grunts and squirrelfish. Other fish, such as the myriad sergeant majors and yellowtail snapper, are conditioned to feeding by divers and will follow you around the wreck. The stern section, including the propeller and rudder can be found nearby in shallower water. Depth at the prop is only about 25 ft (8 m). The long propeller shaft is mostly intact, running

down a gentle slope and still connected to other large components of the wreck. A silver spoon, alleged to have come from the tea cup of Captain Wooley, is encrusted to a piece of metal supporting the shaft, still polished brightly by divers stroking it for good luck.

Great slabs of metal from the hull are strewn along the bottom between the prop and boiler. The second set of

38-39 The hampers and what remains of the superstructures of the Rhone are encrusted by colorful sponges and other similar organisms.

39 left A visit to the Rhone is one of the most unforgettable nocturnal dives of the Caribbean; an excellent opportunity to approach marine animals in a magical scenario with brilliant colors.

39 top right This fascinating view of the Rhone, taken from the bowsprit, requires a very powerful wide-angle lens.

39 center right The Rhone attracts many marine creatures, as this mixed school of grunts and squirrelfish, near the stern.

RMS RHONE

39 bottom right The Rhone's gigantic anchor makes the scene that greets the diver even more fascinating.

deck beams is located in slightly deeper water, off to the right as you swim away from the prop. On top of the twisted metal you can find the famous tools, an enormous set of open-end wrenches.

The *Rhone* has been declared a national park by the British Virgin Islands, protecting the entire wreck and surrounding waters. Moorings are provided, color-coded for dinghies, pleasure craft, and commercial dive boats. A determined diver could tour the entire wreck on one dive, but the *Rhone* is better enjoyed during at least two dives, one for the bow section and one for the stern. Even then, two dives will only get you familiar with the general layout of the wreck, and divers inevitably return for more.

Diving conditions are usually quite good, with excellent visibility and fairly calm seas. A strong current is frequently present, particularly on the bow section.

ANTILLA

BY EGIDIO TRAINITO

ruba is the westernmost island of the Dutch Antilles, just a few miles off the coast of Venezuela. On May 10, 1940 the *Antilla* was docked across from the northwest coast. The ship, built in Hamburg in 1939, flew the German flag and was used to provision German submarines that patrolled the Atlantic Ocean. About 445 ft (135 m) long, she had a gross tonnage of 4400 tons and was unarmed. That day, Nazi Germany invaded the Netherlands, and the Dutch governors of the island immediately advised the commander of the *Antilla* to hand over the ship and consider himself a prisoner of war. He was given one day to decide how to organize the surrender. As in many other cases, in order to prevent the enemy from taking over the ship, during the night the crew set off some explosives and scuttled her, then used their lifeboats to reach the beach of Aruba, where they turned themselves in to the Dutch authorities. Arrested by the Dutch garrison, the commander and crew of the *Antilla* were interned in a prison camp on the island of Bonaire, where they remained until the end of the war.

Today the *Antilla* is one of the best-known wrecks in the world, and each year thousands of divers come to see her. She is lying on her port side on a sandy floor about 59 ft (18 m) deep, with a portion of the

40 top This period photo shows the Antilla at sea. She was a German cargo ship, put to use as a mother ship for the submarines operating in the Atlantic during World War II.

40 center The drawing shows the Antilla seen from the side and from above, in the period when shewas sunk. The lateral view shows the masts with the loading derricks and the small area occupied by the cabins.

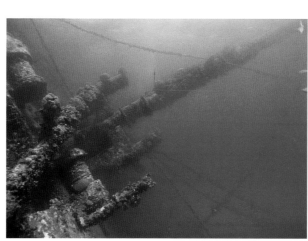

TECHNICAL CARD

TYPE OF WRECK	*Cargo ship*
NATIONALITY	*German*
YEAR OF CONSTRUCTION	*1939*
DATE SUNK	*May 10, 1940*
CAUSE OF SINKING	*Scuttled*
LOCATION	*Aruba, Dutch Antilles*
DISTANCE FROM SHORE	*1 mile / 1.6 Km*
MINIMUM DEPTH	*0 ft / 0 m*
MAXIMUM DEPTH	*59 ft / 18 m*
LENGTH	*about 443 ft / 135 m*

40 bottom
The Antilla *lies on her port side, and the high part of what remains of the mast projects above the surface.*

Stays and braces are still in place, just like the numerous winches that were used to operate the loading derricks.

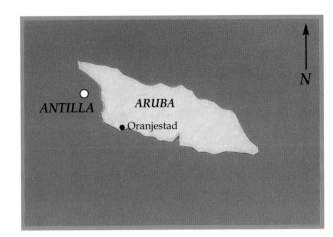

59 ft / 18 m

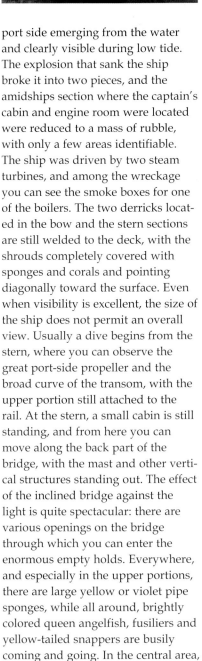

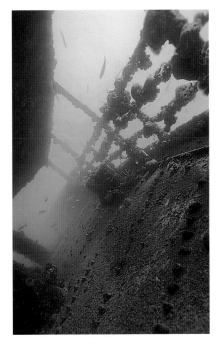

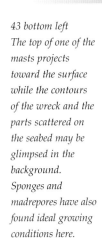

ANTILLA

43 bottom left
The top of one of the masts projects toward the surface while the contours of the wreck and the parts scattered on the seabed may be glimpsed in the background. Sponges and madrepores have also found ideal growing conditions here.

43 bottom right
A large number of marine organisms have found suitable substrata on which to grow on the Antilla, mainly sponge and corals that thrive in areas exposed to currents.

port side emerging from the water and clearly visible during low tide. The explosion that sank the ship broke it into two pieces, and the amidships section where the captain's cabin and engine room were located were reduced to a mass of rubble, with only a few areas identifiable. The ship was driven by two steam turbines, and among the wreckage you can see the smoke boxes for one of the boilers. The two derricks located in the bow and the stern sections are still welded to the deck, with the shrouds completely covered with sponges and corals and pointing diagonally toward the surface. Even when visibility is excellent, the size of the ship does not permit an overall view. Usually a dive begins from the stern, where you can observe the great port-side propeller and the broad curve of the transom, with the upper portion still attached to the rail. At the stern, a small cabin is still standing, and from here you can move along the back part of the bridge, with the mast and other vertical structures standing out. The effect of the inclined bridge against the light is quite spectacular: there are various openings on the bridge through which you can enter the enormous empty holds. Everywhere, and especially in the upper portions, there are large yellow or violet pipe sponges, while all around, brightly colored queen angelfish, fusiliers and yellow-tailed snappers are busily coming and going. In the central area,

42 The bow of the Antilla has split off, in the stokehold area.

43 top left The winches used to lift the anchors are still perfectly recognizable.

43 top center The Antilla's iron bridge is in good condition and may be visited by divers.

43 top right The wreck has broken near the engine room, and many parts are still scattered on the seabed.

the crack in the stern section forms a large cavity where a school of dozens of silvery snappers swims. Going toward the bow, the scene is once again enlivened by the great derrick pointing toward the surface: here you may meet a tortoise swimming lazily along the bridge. At the stern, the large capstans used to maneuver the anchor can be seen, anchor chain still in place. The chain emerges from the hawse-hole and seems to disappear in the sand, but just follow that direction for about 131 ft (40 m), and you'll find the great anchor, still in the same working position it was in when the ship went down.

SCAPA FLOW

BY THOMAS EASOP

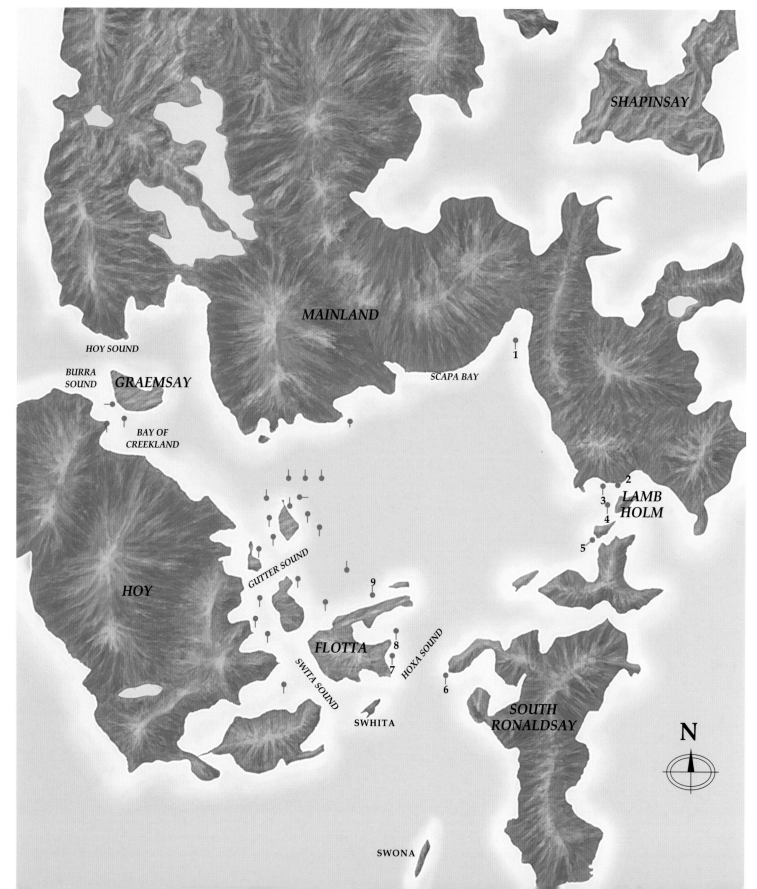

1) **HMS Royal Oak**
2) Numidian
3) Gambhira
4) Tabarka
5) Reginald
6) James Barrie
7) S 54
8) UB 116
9) Concrete Barge
10) Vanguard
11) Prudentha
12) Roedan
13) Imbat
14) B 109
15) F2 VC 21
16) M.T.B
17) V 83
18) Seydlitz
19) S 36
20) Karlsruhe
21) Bayern
22) **SMS Brummer**
23) **SMS Cöln**
24) **SMS Kronprinz Wilhelm**
25) Markgraf
26) König
27) Dresden
28) Gobernador Bories
29) Moyle
30) Inverlane
31) Bremse

45 top The road called Churchill Causeway connects South Ronaldsay to Pasmona, in the Orkneys, north of Scotland, through a continuous sequence of coastlines and long bridges.

45 bottom This period photograph from 1919 shows the most important ships of the Imperial German Navy, anchored in the bay of Scapa Flow.

Labels on map: SHAPINSAY, MAINLAND, HOY SOUND, BURRA SOUND, GRAEMSAY, BAY OF CREEKLAND, SCAPA BAY, LAMB HOLM, HOY, GUTTER SOUND, FLOTTA, SWITA SOUND, HOXA SOUND, SWHITA, SOUTH RONALDSAY, SWONA, N

Scapa Flow is an extensive deep-water harbor situated at the heart of the small archipelago of the Orkney Islands, 12 miles (20 Km) north of the furthermost tip of Scotland, near John O'Groats. The home of hardy farmers and fishers, these islands enclose a roughly circular sheet of water which offers perfect shelter from the gales which frequently rage over the North Sea.

A home to seafarers since the time of the Vikings, Scapa Flow was also the main anchorage for the British Royal Navy for most of the 20th century.

At the end of the Great War it was to hold the interned German Imperial High Seas Fleet. Immediately at the end of hostilities, the Allies demanded the surrender of the 74 war ships as a good-will measure, until the formal signing of the Treaty of Versailles, which took place the following year (1919).

Learning that their ships would be war booty, Admiral von Reuter and his officers worked out a plan to scuttle the entire fleet before the time agreed for their surrender. And so in the afternoon of 21 June 1919, the order was given for the greatest naval "suicide" in history.

The small Royal Navy force on guard at Scapa Flow desperately attempted to prevent the scuttling of the German ships, but was able to save very few. At sunset most of the fleet lay on the seabed. At that point, the British Ministry of War decided to yield the salvage rights to several private companies.

With ingenuity and determination, the salvers brought up all the largest ships, except for seven, which still lie in the depths of Scapa Flow. The most valuable metal was salvaged from the largest of these, while their wrecks were left on the seabed, where they still lie. It was not possible to entirely raise the other four warships, all cruisers, but some parts of them were salvaged.

In order to protect the Royal Navy during the Second World War, several ships were sunk in five narrow sounds separating the isles forming Scapa Flow.

While the wider sounds were protected by anti-submarine nets, mines and patrol forces, in the smaller sounds 43 "blockships" were placed to prevent entry into the harbor.

47 top The last crew members get ready to abandon a torpedo-boat, just before it sinks.

47 center The relic of the Reginald; it was sunk in Est Weddel Sound to create a dangerous naval barrier.

47 bottom The Busk also was sunk in the waters of Scapa Flow, more precisely, in Kirk Sound, to obstruct the access to the channels.

Although the tides in these small sounds were extremely dangerous, especially with the blockship barriers, on the morning of October 14, 1939 the U-47 succeeded in passing ten of them in Kirk Sound and in penetrating unopposed into the natural harbor. HMS *Royal Oak* was immediately torpedoed at her moorings and sunk within eight minutes, taking 833 British sailors to their graves.

All these wrecks, with the exception of the *Royal Oak*, are today an attraction for scuba divers. The sheltered waters of Scapa Flow provide a good number of destinations to explore these historic seabeds. The divers, reaching Orkney on holiday, are the temporary guests of the windy archipelago. The main base is the town of Stromness, from which a dozen boats leave for the dive centers. In the town there are also stores and repair shops for diving equipment.

HMS ROYAL OAK

BY THOMAS EASOP

T he HMS *Royal Oak* was sunk by torpedo on October 14, 1939, just six weeks into World War II, with a staggering loss of 833 British sailors. The last capital ship scheduled to vacate Scapa Flow, she remained to provide temporary anti-aircraft defense of the radio station at Kirkwall. She was designated as a war grave in 2002 but for decades Orkney Harbor bylaws have prohibeted unofficial diving on her.

The wreck of the HMS *Royal Oak* is not a static wreck. Her steelworks have been deteriorating slowly, like many shipwrecks, and she is slowly leaking her fuel oil. Contract divers who are permitted to work on the wreck report that most of her smaller guns still point up, the way they were

when the ship was sunk, defending the sky above Orkney. Her large main armament guns can also be seen, as well as the places where she is leaking oil. She lies almost upside-down on the seabed in 98 ft (30 m) of salt water. Her valuable propellers were salvaged after the war. Since she rises to within almost five meters of the surface there is a large buoy noting the hazard to shipping which also bears a memorial plaque. Each year on October 14, the anniversary of her sinking, a team of Royal Navy divers descend to her and place an ensign on her upside-down hull.

48-49 The officers' lifeboat can be glimpsed in the cloudy waters.

48 top A few drops of fuel oil leak from the encrusted surface.

49 left Sea life flourishes among the relics in Burra Sound.

49 top right The crew of the HMS Royal Oak, portrayed on the ship's deck.

49 bottom right The HMS Royal Oak in a photo from 1939, along with other British men-of-war.

SMS BRUMMER

BY THOMAS EASOP

SMS *Brummer* is the only wreck of a fast mine-laying cruiser in the German High Seas Fleet remaining at Scapa Flow.

It mounted two 150-mm guns and two anti-zeppelin guns and carried 200 mines. The *Brummer* is relatively small, and only 453 ft (138 m) long. She lies on her right side in salt water, at a maximum depth of 118 ft (36 m).

Diving down towards the seabed on the bow side, you can see one of the main 150-mm guns, while the beams and ribs of the now deteriorating hull are silhouetted against the bright blue of the

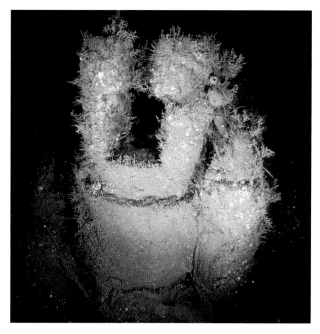

sea above. Swimming aft, you will see the gun deck and main deck. The railings on the deck are still in place, and give a sense of scale. Further on, the ship is collapsing and almost touches the seabed. Below the deck you will find the two anti-aircraft guns, one with its shield upturned, and still intact. Moving aft, you pass alongside the searchlight mounting and the stern mast. A considerable part of the hull has been blasted away by an explosion, revealing the engine room, but hides one of the stern guns from view. Further on, after the last main gun, the only capstan may be seen. The stern itself is disintegrating, enabling the light stern anchor to be seen.

50 top The SMS Brummer was a rapid cruiser and mine-layer in the German fleet. She was equipped with six guns and 200 mines.

50 center Part of the carriage of one of the four 150-mm guns the ship was armed with is visible in this detail.

50 bottom "Only" 453 ft (138 m) long and with limited armor, the Brummer was relatively small but was agile and fast.

51 top A diver, protected from the cold by a watertight wet suit, carefully explores the relic of the Brummer.

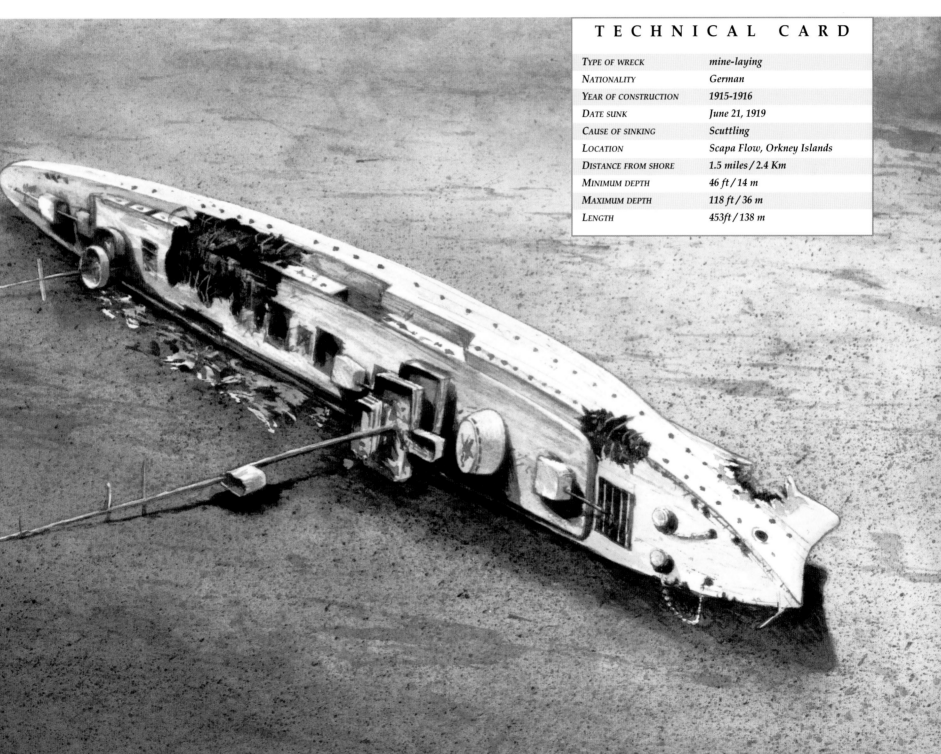

TECHNICAL CARD

TYPE OF WRECK	mine-laying
NATIONALITY	German
YEAR OF CONSTRUCTION	1915-1916
DATE SUNK	June 21, 1919
CAUSE OF SINKING	Scuttling
LOCATION	Scapa Flow, Orkney Islands
DISTANCE FROM SHORE	1.5 miles / 2.4 Km
MINIMUM DEPTH	46 ft / 14 m
MAXIMUM DEPTH	118 ft / 36 m
LENGTH	453ft / 138 m

SMS CÖLN

BY THOMAS EASOP

SMS *Cöln* is one of the two light cruisers scuttled in Scapa Flow by Admiral von Reuter.

The ship was fitted with light 150-mm guns, two anti-aircraft guns and four torpedo tubes. The Cöln is a fairly large 508 ft (155 m) wreck, and lies on her starboard side, at a depth of 112 ft (34 m) in the salt water.

Reaching the side of the ship, if you swim towards the bow, you will find one of the main guns, no longer intact. The barrel has been detached from both its mount and shield.

Above the wreck side may be found the main deck and gun deck, with a heavy armored door at the side and a range finder on deck.

The anchor hawser pipe, with the anchor cut clearly visible, is situated at the bow end of the cruiser.

Halfway between the pipe and seabed, if you swim aft, you will find the twin gun pedestals; the guns are missing; they have been salvaged.

Further on past the decks, you come across a single torpedo tube with a remaining anti-aircraft gun, still attached to the deck. The superstructure has entirely collapsed, and this gun is the only one left to testify to the original appearance of the ship.

Swimming on, you pass an enormous hole opened by an explosion; particular care must be taken at this point, because it is easy to lose your bearings.

Swimming alongside the wreck on the seabed, you will see a searchlight mounting and the stern guns. Since the rear part of the Cöln is still intact, both these two guns are very well preserved.

TYPE OF WRECK	*Light cruiser*
NATIONALITY	*German*
YEAR OF CONSTRUCTION	*1915-1918*
DATE SUNK	*June 21, 1919*
CAUSE OF SINKING	*Scuttling*
LOCATION	*Scapa Flow, Orkney Islands*
DISTANCE FROM SHORE	*1 mile / 1.6 Km*
MINIMUM DEPTH	*46 ft / 14 m*
MAXIMUM DEPTH	*119 ft / 36 m*
LENGTH	*535 ft / 153 m*

52 top The SMS Cöln, sunk on the order of Admiral Reuter, was 535 ft (153 m) long light cruisers.

52 bottom left The main deck and the battle deck of the light cruiser are still in relatively good shape.

53 top The SMS Cöln lies on the seabed at a depth of 119 ft (36 m), reclined on its right side.

53 center Only an anti-aircraft rapid fire gun is still visible on deck, along with a torpedo tube.

53 bottom The ship was armed with eight 150-mm guns, two anti-zeppelin guns and four torpedo tubes.

SMS KRONPRINZ WILHELM

BY THOMAS EASOP

SMS *Kronprinz Wilhelm* is the wreck of one of the three König-class battleships scuttled in Scapa Flow by the Germans. Each of these ships mounted ten 300-mm naval guns, two for each turret, which, five in number, were all located along the central line of the ship. In addition, 14 other guns were protected by casemates. At some points the armor plate was over 30 cm thick.

It is advisable to explore the wreck, which lies upside down, from the stern. Diving down to the seabed and swimming along the lower part of the hull, pointing towards the surface, the stern turrets may be seen. The most aft one has remained suspended above the seabed, while its guns are hidden by the deck, which is deteriorating relentlessly and now about to detach from the wreck.

The second turret is buried in the sand and the port-side gun is lying on the seabed. Ascending along the wreck side, you come to two casemate guns, half-hidden in the wreckage. The metal core of these casement guns is now uncovered, because the armor belt protecting them has completely collapsed. It is easy to inspect them, and also of interest since it is a rare opportunity to examine parts of a wreck which are usually hidden.

Descending towards the seabed from the foremost casemate, it is possible to see the armor belt.

A window in the armor is aligned with the gun above. At this point of the wreck the three layers making up the armor belt may clearly be seen.

Swimming towards the bow, you will note the barrels of all seven casemate guns, placed at regular intervals on the port side. From here, continuing towards the bow, you may find an entry passage near the seabed, which leads to an opened turret buried in the sand. Inside you may see various pieces of machinery and the breech of a 300-mm gun.

Under the bow deck the barrel of the main gun can be seen, with the anchor chain still wrapped around it. This section of the wreck is often inhabited by lobsters.

54 The SMS Kronprinz Wilhelm was sunk along with two other armored ships at Scapa Flow in 1919 (the photograph shows her on a cruise before the battle of Jutland). It was armed with ten 300-mm naval guns and 14 guns protected by blockhouses.

55 top left As the ship lies on her back, it is possible to observe only the after turrets by swimming below the hull. The far aft turret is suspended upside down above the seabed.

55 top right Proceeding toward the bow, a passage leads to a turret revealing machinery and the butt of a 300-mm gun.

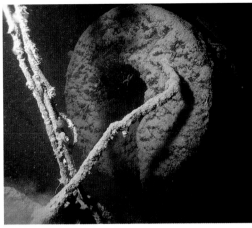

TECHNICAL CARD

TYPE OF WRECK	*Battleship*
NATIONALITY	*German*
YEAR OF CONSTRUCTION	*1912-1914*
DATE SUNK	*June 21, 1919*
CAUSE OF SINKING	*Scuttling*
LOCATION	*Scapa Flow, Orkney Islands*
DISTANCE FROM SHORE	*0.75 miles / 1.2 Km*
MINIMUM DEPTH	*46 ft / 14 m*
MAXIMUM DEPTH	*125 ft / 38 m*
LENGTH	*567 ft / 173 m*

MEDITER

BY EGIDIO TRAINITO

The Mediterranean is a closed sea, but that's not the only thing that makes it so special. Although it is small compared to the great oceans, navigation is often difficult and dangerous. Yet man has always crossed it in increasingly sophisticated vessels.

It is also a sea in continuous transformation. Its average level over the past 18,000 years has risen by about 360ft (110 m); 2000 years ago it was about 3 ft (1 m) lower than today. Great rivers discharge their waters into this small sea, profoundly changing many coastal areas: suffice it to consider the Nile, the Rhône, the Po, and the Danube, which last flows into the Black Sea.

The constant changes in the coastline explain the extraordinary discoveries of ancient ships from Pisa a long way from the sea, and perhaps also the discovery of 24 ancient ships from Olbia, sunk at their moorings in an ancient port that no longer exists. While these ships are exceptional, as they were discovered buried under changed shorelines, the Mediterranean is a cauldron of history, only part of which has been erased by the waves and time. In fact, there are thousands of known ancient and modern shipwrecks, and hundreds of thousands about which we know nothing.

There is an impressive number of known ships in this underwater museum preserved by the Mediterranean. Most of them are the result of the two world wars. Suffice it to note that in World War II alone, the Italian merchant fleet lost 2886

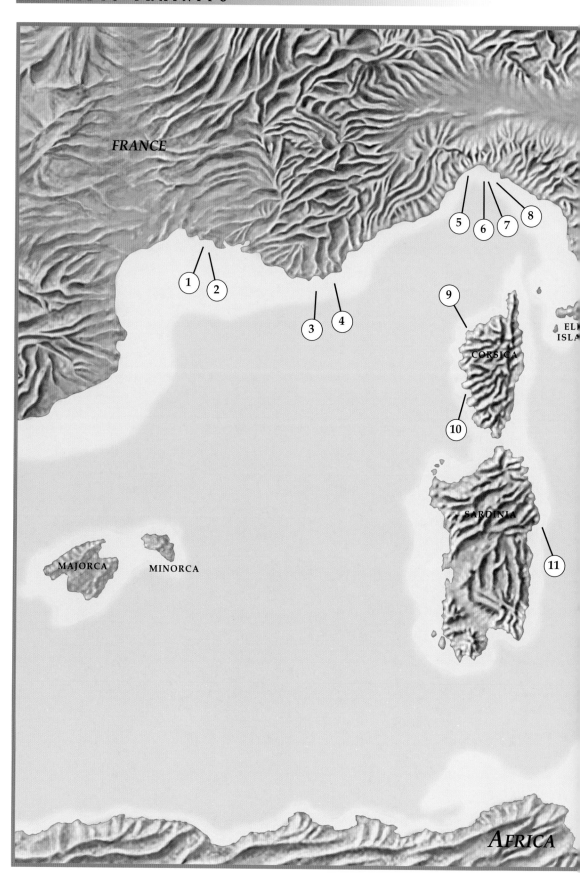

RANEAN SEA

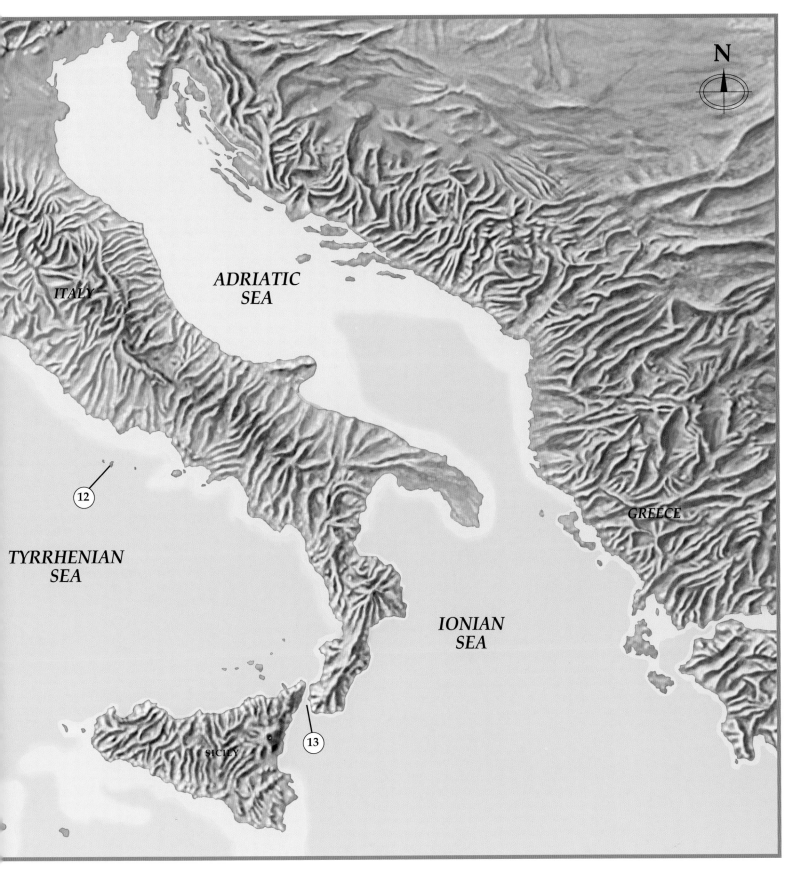

ITALY

ADRIATIC
SEA

TYRRHENIAN
SEA

⑫

GREECE

IONIAN
SEA

SICILY

⑬

N

1) LIBAN

2) MESSERSCHMITT 109

3) PROSPERO SCHIAFFINO

4) RUBIS

5) HAVEN

6) GENOVA

7) SESTRI KT

8) SESTRI ARMED
   CARGO SHIP

9) B-17 E

10) VICKERS VIKING

11) KT 12

12) LST

13) LAURA C

MEDITERRANEAN SEA

ships, while the military reported the loss of 1103 units. If we note that these are data for only a five-year period (1940-1945) and only for Italian ships, we get an idea of how many shipwrecks the Mediterranean may contain. And while boats are the most common, all kinds of wrecks, including hundreds of airplanes that crashed into the sea, can be found here. This book contains descriptions of three of them. In the Adriatic, even a methane platform, the *Paguro*, has become a scuba-diving site.

The fact that war is the major cause of Mediterranean shipwrecks becomes evident not only from this book, where of the thirteen wrecks described, only five are non-military in origin, but also from the location of known wrecks in the sea, all concentrated in strategic areas. The most common locations are the coast of Provence and Liguria, followed by Sardinia, where most of the many wrecks occurred in the fatal year of 1943 during World War II. In these two areas, diving on wrecks is a tradition of underwater tourism, and thousands of enthusiasts can conveniently relive the thrill of discovery. Just as extraordinary is the concentration of warships along the North African coast of Tunisia and Libya, the theater of one of the most important fronts in World War II.

Unlike the previous areas, however, most of these wrecks have been located on nautical charts only, often in approximate positions, and have not yet entered the circuits of underwater tourism. Another very important area is the Aegean Sea between the southern coast of the Peloponnesus and the island of Crete: but the wrecks here are in very deep water and many have yet to be discov-

ered. Moreover, owing to local regulations intended to protect the extraordinary ancient archaeological heritage of the Greek seas, only now have restrictions on scuba diving become less stringent.

Along with the war wrecks on the following pages, you'll also find the most famous peacetime wreck, the *Haven*, an oil tanker that held coastal inhabitants with bated breath as it threatened to pollute the northern Tyrrhenian coast. Today these fears have faded, and the ship has become not only an extraordinary receptacle of marine life, as pictures show better than a thousand words, but also a popular tourist stop.

Diving on Mediterranean wrecks is possible year round, due in part to an extensive tourist structure. Water temperature never goes below 11° to 12° C (52° to 54° F) even in winter, and in the summer tends to be around 24°-25° degrees even in deep water, especially in the central and southern Mediterranean. Visibility is better in the summer than in the winter, while currents are generally intermittent.

58 The wreck of a French Corsair *airplane lies on the floor of the bay of Capo Comino, Sardinia. Partially buried in the sand, the remains of the airplane hold a mystery: human remains were found inside it, but the French air force declared that the pilot had been rescued.*

59 bottom The extraordinary concentration of crinoids of every hue almost seems like the Haven's revenge for the predictions of environmental apocalypse that followed her sinking in 1991 off the coast of Arenzano in the Ligurian Sea.

LIBAN

BY KURT AMSLER

T he sinking of the passenger steamship the *Liban*, which took the lives of almost 200 people, was the greatest maritime catastrophe that the port city of Marseilles in southern France had ever experienced. Due perhaps to a storm, poor visibility, or even a breakdown, the *Liban*, loaded with passengers on their way to Corsica, unexpectedly collided with a steamship — the *Insulaire*.

The two ships sighted each other near the island of Tiboulen de Mairé.

As they were at a safe distance of about 328 ft (100 m), the captains decided to cross, and gave the order to heave to starboard.

In the open sea, it was such a simple maneuver! And in fact the *Liban* turned with no problems. But the *Insulaire* had to deal with the island, which was dangerously close. To avoid smashing against the reefs, the captain shouted: "Hard to port!" thus canceling the previous maneuver.

The bow of the *Insulaire* made a deep gash in the starboard side of the *Liban*, smashing the planking beams, which seemed to groan with the tremendous crash. It was exactly 12:30 pm. On board the *Liban*, Captain Lacotte ordered complicated maneuvers to free his ship from the bow of the *Insulaire*. When he managed to disentangle the ship and fully evaluate the consequences of the collision, the captain made an emergency decision to get as close as possible to the island of Mairé and run the ship aground.

But no one expected what hap-

pened next! Just 65 ft (20 m) from the reef that would have saved it, the stern of the *Liban* slowly began to rise above the water's surface.

The ship's propeller continued to churn in the air, the ship began to vibrate, but didn't move at all. Then she began to sink bow first, at first slowly and then with incredible speed.

Everything happened so fast that the crew had no time to prepare the lifeboats.

A horrifying scene followed. Many drowned when they panicked and jumped overboard even though they did not how to swim; and those who could swim were hindered by their drenched clothing. Others sought refuge on the masts or superstructures, but the increasing list of the ship forced them to drop onto the deck or into the waves.

60 top left This photograph of the Insulaire, *taken shortly after the tragedy, clearly shows the bow, heavily damaged by the impact.*

60 top right
A period illustration shows a reconstruction of the tragedy: the Liban *sinks in a few minutes, the bow first, and the crew did not even have time to launch the lifeboats.*

60 bottom This *bronze sculpture of a lady and the bronze mortar certainly adorned one of the salons of the* Liban.

LA CATASTROPHE DU « LIBAN »
Le sauvetage des passagers

Marseille

RATONNEAU

POMÈGUES

FRANCE

MAIRE   CAP CROISETTE

LE PLANIER

LIBAN   N

98 ft / 30 m

118 ft / 36 m

TECHNICAL CARD

TYPE OF WRECK	Passenger steamship
NATIONALITY	French
YEAR OF CONSTRUCTION	1882
DATE SUNK	July 6, 1903
CAUSE OF SINKING	Collision with the steamship Insulaire
LOCATION	In front of Les Farillons, France
DISTANCE FROM SHORE	66 ft / 20 m
MINIMUM DEPTH	98 ft / 30 m
MAXIMUM DEPTH	118 ft / 36 m
LENGTH	295 ft / 90 m

Many ships who were alerted rushed to the scene of the tragedy.

Sailors feverishly lowered lifeboats, seeking to the rescue people in the water.

Sadly, in this total chaos, it was impossible to properly organize the rescue of those who remained on the ship, nor those floundering in the waves.

Suddenly, there was a tremendous explosion: the compressed air boiler of the steam engine had exploded with an ear-splitting roar, creating powerful jets of water and steam: the *Liban* literally snapped in two amidships.

Soon, the bubbling waves closed like a deadly curtain over the ship that had bravely plied these waters.

The area where the wreck is located, near Les Farillons, is well-protected from northern winds, but is swept by winds form the south and east, which create billowing waves.

The 295 ft (90 m) long *Liban* is located at depths of 98 ft (30 m) (the bow) and 118 ft (36 m) (the stern).

It's best to start the dive at the stern, which, as is generally the case for vessels with a keel, is inclined 45° from the sea floor. As you approach, the details of the wreck begin to emerge: first you'll see the elegant silhouette of the quarter-deck, and on it the steering gear.

Following the bulwark down to the rudder, you can see the bronze propeller deeply embedded in the

sand. Here, on the side in the shadows, the vessel is richly covered in luxuriant gorgonians that in the light of the underwater torches shine with magnificent deep red tones. Going up from here, you will gradually come to the bow of the ship.

After the stern section, which is still in good condition, you will swim past a mass of metal, then you'll come to the enormous compressed air boiler of the steam engine, partially gutted by the explosion. Near this great tank, which was responsible for sinking the ship, you'll see more devastating damage.

When swimming against the current, the superstructures offer divers a good shelter.

A myriad of damselfish (*Heliastes chromis*) now live in the ship's old saloon, and dense schools of snappers swim through pathways in the planking; great conger eels with bulging eyes, attracted by the light, peep out of the contorted wreckage. You'll never grow tired of admiring the vegetation that covers this wreck and observing the abundance of marine creatures who have chosen to live here. While the deeper sections are the realm of red gorgonians, on the deck, the garden of sea fans is gold, covering the metal supports and winding into the passageways.

Once here, the deck appears almost flat, and the massive capstan

that hoisted the anchor is still facing the bow.

From this position you have a magnificent view that spans the rail of the port-side bulwark (with the davits that launched the lifeboats) to the bow, significantly raised, to one of the masts, which like many other parts of the wreck lies to starboard on the sandy seabed.

62 left The stern of the wreck lies at a depth of 118 ft (36 m).

62 right The starboard side, facing north, is covered by large red gorgonias.

63 top left The image shows the Liban's foredeck. After 102 years on the seabed, the wooden boards of the bridge have rotted completely, revealing the iron structure.

63 center top The davits supporting the lifeboats are visible on the Liban's tall bow.

63 top right Two intact steam boilers are still visible in the central area of the ship.

63 bottom The powerful winch on the foredeck is now home to yellow gorgonians.

MESSERSCHMITT 109

BY KURT AMSLER

65 top left The island of Le Planier lies south-east of Marseilles; the wreck lies just at 328 ft (100 m) from the impressive lighthouse.

Marseille

RATONNEAU

FRANCE

POMÈGUES

MESSERSCHMITT 109

CAPE CROISETTE

LE PLANIER

MAIRE

N

144 ft / 44 m

151 ft / 46 m

O n March 7, 1944, the air-raid alarm sounded at the Istre military air base near Avignon.

Two American B-17 bombers escorted by two Lightning fighter planes were approaching the port city of Marseilles.

To stop the enemy planes, two fearsome German Messerschmitt ME109 fighters took off. One of the pilots was Captain Hans Fahrenberger, who almost lost his life in the mission. The German pilots soon sighted the American bombers, and immediately launched an attack in their Messerschmitts.

Captain Fahrenberger swooped down and began spraying bullets at the enemy formation from the 30-mm-cannon installed in the propeller boss.

But he missed his target, because his plane was being buffeted by such strong gusts of wind that it shifted position.

In order to launch another attack, he once again pointed the nose up and rose vertically.

But the engine suddenly stopped.

Due to the high altitude and strong wind, the pilot was nevertheless able to glide for miles and miles.

The two American Lightning fighters left him to his fate: having seen the smoke rising from the engine of the Messerschmitt, which continued to lose altitude, they had given him up for dead.

But despite the strong wind, the skilled pilot managed to direct his plane toward the little island of Le Planier, marked by a lighthouse, and make make a water landing about 328 ft (100 m) from the shoals. Amidst great jets of spray, a blade of the propeller broke off like a matchstick, while the aircraft's metal plate folded like cardboard.

In just a few seconds, the plane sank like a stone, but the captain managed to open the roof and return

65 right The Messerschmitt 109, here photographed while on two missions during World War II, was the Luft waffe's finest fighter in the early 1940s.

TECHNICAL CARD	
TYPE OF WRECK	Fighter plane
NATIONALITY	German
YEAR OF CONSTRUCTION	Unknown
DATE SUNK	March 7, 1944
CAUSE OF SINKING	Engine breakdown
LOCATION	North of Le Planier Island, France
DISTANCE FROM SHORE	328 ft / 100 m
MINIMUM DEPTH	144 ft / 44 m
MAXIMUM DEPTH	151 ft / 46 m
LENGTH	About 30 ft / 9 m

to the surface with the aid of a para-chute, whose buoyancy gave him a lucky thrust upward.

The pilot, who swam to Le Planier, was sighted the next day by a German patrol ship, which took him on board safe and sound.

The wreck of the Messerschmitt lies at a depth of 45 meters, about 100 meters from Le Planier Island.

In truth, it is only 28.7 ft (8.74 m) long, with a wing span of 32.3 ft (9.86 m), so it's not easy to find. You can moor directly above the wreck or begin your dive from the island itself. If you do, you'll also be able to admire the luxuriant red gorgonians that adorn the north-facing reefs.

If the current is not strong, you'll quickly reach a rise along the rocky wall, right at the level of the first window of the lighthouse building. From there, heading exactly 0° to the north on the sloping sand, you'll need to swim 150 ft (45 m).

The silhouette of the dive bomber can be seen even from a distance, looking something like a monstrous insect with its legs in the air — the aircraft is in fact lying upside down, with the landing gear facing up. One of the blades of the propeller of the powerful 2000 PS engine, which enabled the Messerschmitt to fly at a speed of 450 mph (727 kmphr), was driven into the sand, while the others are broken.

The tail and tail unit are slightly curved, a reminder of the futile attempts by professional scuba divers to move the wreck in order to coax the secrets of its cockpit out into the open.

The wreck, which rests on a broad stretch of sand, has become a true garden — an oasis. Several eels have now found a home in the muzzle of the 30 mm cannon mounted on the propeller boss.

The wings and the landing gear are encrusted with sizeable tubificids.

Large lamellibranchs have colonized the metal bracings over the half century they have spent underwater.

Given the small size of the wreck, you should be very careful not to kick up sand from the sea floor, which would immediately reduce visibility.

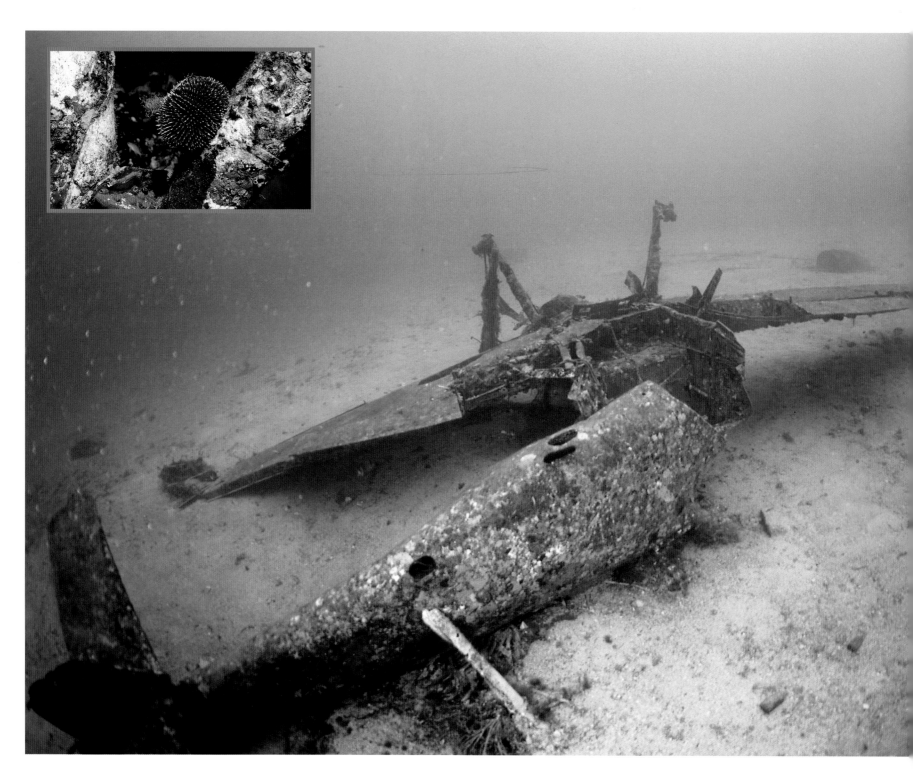

MESSERSCHMITT 109

66 left The Messerschmitt is not just a historical war testimonial; it has also become an artificial reef that houses numerous living creatures, such as this sea-urchin.

66-67 The plane lies on its back on the seabed. The tail broke as a result of an unsuccessful attempt to raise the plane.

67 top Violent impact with the water broke two propeller blades. The remaining one is deeply buried in the sand.

67 center A diver armed with a torch explores the wreck, illuminating the front of the Messerschmitt 109.

67 bottom A diver examines the aircraft's engine, a powerful 2000 PS, with a small 30-mm gun.

PROSPERO SCHIAFFINO

BY ALBERTO VANZO

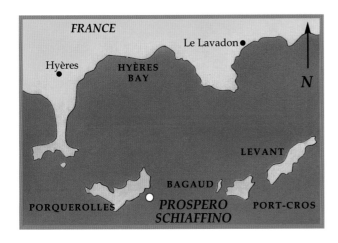

FRANCE

Le Lavadon

Hyères

HYÈRES
BAY

N

LEVANT

BAGAUD

PORQUEROLLES   PROSPERO   PORT-CROS
                    SCHIAFFINO

82 ft / 25 m

167 ft / 51 m

68 bottom
The Prospero
Schiaffino, *launched
in 1931 as* Petit
Terre, *here shown in
a period photo,
became part of the
merchant fleet owned
by shipper Charles
Schiaffino, who used
to change the name of
the ships he acquired,
calling them after his
relatives.*

69 center
The Prospero
Schiaffino *lies on a
sandy seabed at a
depth of 167 ft (51
m) off the island of
Porquerolles, in an
area where the
mistral blows but
where visibility is
good.*

T his ship has a strange story. The nature of its cargo gives it something in common with many other shipwrecks, especially in ancient times, while the reasons it foundered are inevitably related to our times.

This cargo ship, made to transport food, escaped World War II unscathed as it criss-crossed the seas. But she met her end while transporting a load of wine after the war was over, sinking in a mixture of red wine and diesel oil.

The *Prospero Schiaffino*, launched under the name of *Petit Terre* was built in 1931 in one of the Norwegian shipyards in Bergen, owned by the company Holz Werksted A/S. She was a sturdy merchant ship 256 ft (78.28 m) long and 40 ft (11.94 m) wide, with a draught of 18 ft (5.5 m). She was powered by a 1,800-hp engine and her gross tonnage was 1,698 tons. In her early voyages, she transported bananas from the Antilles to France. In 1939, she joined the merchant fleet owned by Charles Schiaffino, who named the ships he acquired after his relatives. The war

69 bottom
*Because of the
strong currents, a
rope fixed to a
floater should be
fixed to the bridge of
the wreck, to
guarantee safe
descents and
ascents.*

TECHNICAL CARD

TYPE OF WRECK	**Merchant ship**
NATIONALITY	**French**
YEAR OF CONSTRUCTION	**1931**
DATE SUNK	**November 10, 1945**
CAUSE OF SINKING	**Struk with a mine**
LOCATION	**South-east of Porquerolles Island, France**
DISTANCE FROM SHORE	**1 mile / 6 km**
MINIMUM DEPTH	**82 ft / 25 m**
MAXIMUM DEPTH	**167 ft / 51 m**
LENGTH	**256 ft / 78 m**

proved fatal to the 20 other ships owned by the company, which were all destroyed or damaged, while Mr. Schiaffino's probable last purchase before the start of hostilities met its end last, after the war was over. In October 1945, the cargo ship left the port of Marseilles to carry vegetables to Algiers, and after taking on a load of red wine, headed out to sea on its way back to Toulon, France. The captain, worried by the fact that minesweeping was not yet complete in the Mediterranean, ordered the crew to be very careful, but his warnings were not enough. On November 10, after the passage between the island of Porquerolles and the Giens peninsula was blocked, the ship changed her usual course and entered the channel that separates Porquerolles from Port-Cros. Here, at 1:10 p.m., in this sea usually swept by the mistral with often powerful currents, the ship's bow hit a drifting mine and sank in just a few minutes. Of the 29 men on board, 25 were rescued, two were never found, and the other two were recovered, but never regained consciousness.

Today, after many years, the sea has absorbed every trace of the pollution created by the wreck, and incessant colonization has transformed a ghost into an underwater garden far richer than many other wrecks in the Mediterranean.

70 top left A large spare propeller, completely encrusted, has remained fixed to the after superstructure.

70-71 The wreck is today completely covered by concretion, and colonized by luxuriant "forests" of red gorgonians (Paramunicea clavata).

70 bottom The contrast between the colorful organisms and encrustation that emerge in the shade of the wreck and the blue background create fascinating vistas.

PROSPERO SCHIAFFINO

With regard to any "wine pollution," the only effect now visible may be the ruby red forests of gorgonians, impressive quantities of which have covered what remains exposed to the current.

Still, the price to pay in order to see this wreck is still rather high, at least in terms of energy. This dive is also recommended for only expert divers. In fact, the combination of very deep water, varying from 167 ft (51 m) at the stern to 157 ft (48 m) at the bow, to less than 131 ft (40 m) in the superstructures, the ship's large size, and the almost constant current, make it impossible to visit the entire wreck at one time. For the first dive, your itinerary could be to descend to the quarterdeck and, after visiting the helm, go to the great propeller and the rudder on the sea floor.

Coming back up among the red and yellow gorgonians that cover this part of the keel and the hull, you can see on the bridgehouse the majestic mast rising up toward the surface.

A second itinerary follows the infrastructures that made up the bridge and crew quarters, in an area of the wreck where the gorgonians are amazingly large and thick.

Proceeding toward the bow, due to the separation of the planks of the deck, you can see many metal barrels loaded in the hold.

The bow area was shaken violently, and among the crevices you'll see a family of sedentary groupers swimming around and patrolling this area, which is certainly less spectacular and more dangerous, due to the distance you must travel to return to the amidships area.

71 top After so long under water, the superstructures of the ship have turned into a metal skeleton covered by numerous gorgonians.

71 bottom left The large red gorgonians, constantly nurtured by the current, have in some cases grown to exceptional dimensions.

RUBIS

BY KURT AMSLER

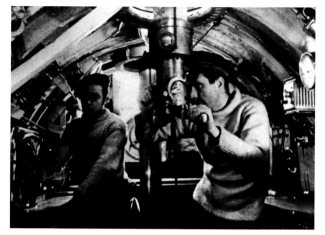

FRANCE

Sainte Maxime •

GULF OF SAINT TROPEZ

CAPE SAINT TROPEZ

Saint Tropez •

CAP CAMARAT

○ *RUBIS*

CAVALAIRE BAY

N

111 ft / 34 m
134 ft / 41 m

TECHNICAL CARD

TYPE OF WRECK	*mine-laying*
NATIONALITY	*German*
YEAR OF CONSTRUCTION	*1931*
DATE SUNK	*January 31, 1958*
CAUSE OF SINKING	*Gunnery target*
LOCATION	*In front of Cap Camarat, France*
DISTANCE FROM SHORE	*1.4 miles / 2.2 km*
MINIMUM DEPTH	*111 ft / 34 m*
MAXIMUM DEPTH	*134 ft / 41 m*
LENGTH	*216 ft / 66 m*

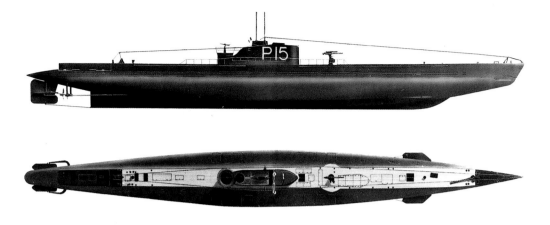

T he French submarine *Rubis* was launched in 1931 and went into service the following year. She was built in the Toulon shipyards, the fourth in a series of six submarines.

The 1930 prototype, the *Saphir,* had been followed by the *Turquoise,* the *Nautilus,* the *Rubis,* the *Diamant,* and, in 1937, the *Perle.*

These six submarines were designed to be able to drop mines in enemy waters without having to resurface; they could also launch torpedoes. All 32 of each submarine's mines were on the outside of the pressurized body, protected by a hydrodynamic shielding. Each vessel had 8 tubes on each side, with two mines in each of them, one above the other.

At the strike site, the *Rubis* released her mines using a compressed air system.

Unlike other types of submarines, which released mines using gates, this model's external system enormously reduced risk.

The mines were manufactured by Sauter and Harley, and each contained 485 lbs (220 kg) of explosive. After being released, these instruments of death automatically rose to the surface, remaining anchored in position by chains. After the mines had been placed, the submarine's ballast had to be adjusted to avoid her resurfacing in enemy waters.

The *Rubis* also had two 75-mm Swiss Bührle-Oerlikon cannons mounted on deck. In order to attack large ships, she was also equipped with five torpedoes; these were launched from the bow.

The *Rubis* had two Vickers-Arm-

72 top The captain of the Rubis, *French Lieutenant Georges Cabanier, scans the horizon with a periscope.*

73 top The construction plans of the Rubis, *the fourth in a series of six submarines, demonstrate its perfect and highly hydrodynamic lines.*

73 center General de Gaulle reviews the equipment of the Rubis, *which fought with the Allied forces until the end of World War II.*

73 bottom This historic image shows the submarine cruising the waters off Toulon. The Rubis *was one of the most efficient submarines in World War II.*

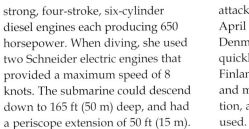

74 The anchor chain hangs from the wreck's streamlined bow.

75 left The platform of the rear turret was rotating and armed with a Swiss Bührle-Oerlikon cannon.

75 top right The turret is still in good condition, though encrusted.

75 bottom right The wreck's stern preserves the two parallel torpedo launchers.

strong, four-stroke, six-cylinder diesel engines each producing 650 horsepower. When diving, she used two Schneider electric engines that provided a maximum speed of 8 knots. The submarine could descend down to 165 ft (50 m) deep, and had a periscope extension of 50 ft (15 m).

At the outbreak of war, all six of the submarines were all based in Toulon. At that time, the French naval command was convinced that France could maintain wartime operations in the strategically important Mediterranean. In January 1940, the French admiralty received its first operational orders. Allied operation were intended to support Finland in case it was attacked by the Soviet Union. But on April 9, the German army occupied Denmark and Norway. Allied forces quickly began to mine the waters off Finland to block the transport of iron and metals. To facilitate this operation, all available submarines were used.

The *Rubis*, commanded by Lieutenant Georges Cabanier, thus operated in the Baltic until France capitulated. She then passed under the English flag. With the same crew, she then fought for the Resistance. In the course of 28 operations, the *Rubis* laid 683 mines. After the war, analyses made of documentary evidence presented the *Rubis'* achievement as follows:

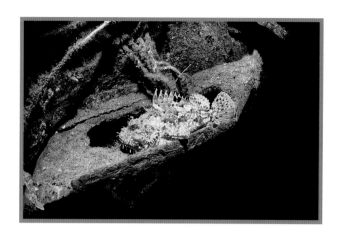

15 support ships sunk
7 destroyer-submarines sunk
1 submarine seriously damaged
1 cargo ship with a gross tonnage of 4360 tons sunk

At the end of the war, the *Rubis* returned to her station in Toulon, and the crew received the highest military French and English honors. The *Rubis* was then completely over-hauled, and for many years the French navy used her to train crews.

In 1958, in order to avoid having to demolish this renowned submarine, she was sunk with full honors across from Cap Camarat, between Cavalaire and St. Tropez.

In this way, an important page of history was preserved for posterity and an extraordinarily interesting wreck was created for scuba divers.

The *Rubis* now rests upright in 131 ft (40 m) of water, as if she had been expressly placed in that position on the sandy sea floor. When the water is clear, you can see the menacing silhouette of the submarine from just a few meters below the surface. Yet, as in all submarine wrecks, something hostile and mysterious seems to creep into your soul as you approach the *Rubis*. Given her erect position, resting on her keel, it almost seems that like half a century ago, she is lying in ambush for her enemy and could suddenly start her engines and silently glide off into the deep blue sea.

The wreck is still in good condition, although a few structures — the turret, the cannon platform and the covering of the mine traps — are slowly falling into decay, corroded by the sea and time. No especially luxuriant vegetation covers the *Rubis* like it does the *Togo,* which lies nearby. Still, gorgonians and sponges live on its sides, while the mains, crevices and niches offer shelter to many large conger eels, morays and scorpionfish.

However, it is not just the proliferation of plant life or profusion of fish that make this wreck so compelling. Before your eyes you'll see the turret, the mine tubes, the torpedo launchers, the diving rudder, and the cable shearer on the bow, evoking the past splendor of the submarine, which after so many missions ended on the seabed sea.

To plan a totally safe dive, you'll need the following information: the *Rubis* is 215 ft/66 m long, and she can thus be visited completely in one dive. Entering the submarine from the narrow hatch is not recommended. First of all, the narrow opening will not allow a large tank or two small ones to pass through, and in addition, visibility inside the hull would be extremely low due to sediments. At Cap Camarat, the current can become quite powerful during certain periods of the year and times of day. Take this factor into consideration when planning your dive.

HAVEN

BY VINCENZO PAOLILLO

TECHNICAL CARD

TYPE OF WRECK	Oil tanker
NATIONALITY	Greek - (under Liberian flag)
YEAR OF CONSTRUCTION	1973
DATE SUNK	April 14, 1991
CAUSE OF SINKING	Fire
LOCATION	Punta di San Martino, Italy
DISTANCE FROM SHORE	1 mile / 1.6 km
MINIMUM DEPTH	108 ft / 33 m
MAXIMUM DEPTH	295 ft / 90 m
LENGTH	820 ft / 250 metres

ITALY

N

Arenzano

GULF OF
GENOA

HAVEN

108 ft / 33 m

295 ft / 90 m

When the Arab-Israeli conflict led to the closing of the Suez Canal and it became necessary to circumnavigate Africa to reach Europe from the Middle East, the large oil shippers began building enormous oil tankers.

The *Amoco Milford,* the first in a series of four identical ships, was built in the Cadiz shipyards and delivered to Amoco in 1973. The ship was 1096 ft (334 m) long and 167 ft (51 m) wide and had 14 tanks, holding a total of over 230,000 tons of crude. She was powered by a 30,000-hp diesel engine, which enabled her to reach 15 knots when fully loaded.

In 1985 the *Amoco Milford* was sold to the Haven Maritime Corporation of Monrovia and renamed the *Haven,* a name she retained when purchased by another Liberian company, which concealed her real ownership by the Haji brothers, who were Greek shipowners.

In 1988, during the Iraq-Iran War, the ship was attacked by an Iranian frigate and sustained serious damage.

*79 In the days
between 11 and 14
April 1991, the
Haven burned,
raising an enormous
column of smoke.*

80 top A diver explores the windows of the Haven's bridge already encrusted and covered with extraordinary marine flora and fauna.

80-81 We can see the enormous smokestack cut off at 33 meters deep so as not create an obstacle for large ships that more through the area.

81 top In the second stage of colonization, feather stars (Antedon mediterranea) covered the entire ship. The large hoist covered by feather stars can be seen to the right.

81 center Schools of red anthias (Anthias anthias) are found everyone, on the smokestacks, on the decks and on the ladders.

81 bottom A diver lights the roof in front of the large mast on which a complicated system of pipes stands.

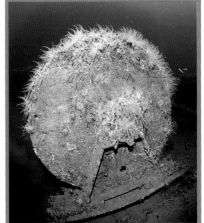

She was towed to Singapore, and more than three months were needed for repairs on her boilers, engine, and rudder. In late 1990 she went to sea again, ironically under lease to an Iranian oil company who manned her with Greek officers and a Filipino crew.

In March 1991, the *Haven,* carrying about 224,000 tons of Iranian crude, circumnavigated Africa and on March 8 arrived at Genoa, where she unloaded part of its cargo at a float-ing islands terminal. She then docked in the harbor to await orders.

On the morning of April 11, the *Haven* began a routine operation, the transshipment of a portion of her cargo in order to adjust her draft. A violent explosion rocked the forward tanks, followed a few minutes later by another at the stern, causing an enormous fire. Firefighters immediately fought the blaze, but they could do nothing against the fire. It ignited the oil, which spilled into the sea. Only 31 members of the crew were saved. Three others were reduced to human torches in an instant, and the bodies of two more, including the captain, were never found.

That night, as the ship continued to burn and lose enormous amounts of crude, she began to list. At this point, some technical experts favored dragging her out as far as possible and sinking her in the high seas. Others felt it would be better to tow the tanker out to shallow waters, close to the coast, to facilitate future clean-up efforts.

The port commander, Admiral Alati, wisely opted for the second solution, and the ship was towed. When she was in about 1,640 ft (500 m) of water, there was another violent explosion: the *Haven* had lost her shield and about 190 ft (80 m) of her forward section. She was towed to the coast until she reached the stretch of sea across from the promontory of Punta S. Martino, between Arenzano and Cogoleto.

There, on the morning of April 14, after two days of intense concern as large amounts of oil spilled into the sea, the fire suddenly went out. Shortly thereafter, enveloped in a cloud of smoke, the ship went down, leaving huge oil slicks on the surface.

But the emergency was not over. Much of the crude had burned, but much remained on the surface. Despite prompt intervention, the deployment of other vessels, and the unusual use of floating booms to contain the spill, oil flowed over local beaches, causing incalculable damage.

Since then, the *Haven* has remained perfectly upright on a sea floor 178 ft (75m) in depth. Throughout the lengthy criminal proceedings, which ended with acquittal of the prosecuted parties, diving on the *Haven* was the privilege of few. Now it is freely permitted, and various buoys anchored to the deck lead to the enormous smokestack and the rear section, making the dive safer and reducing the possible recurrence of the serious accidents that have occurred in past years. Nonetheless, this is a dive for truly skilled, expert divers. The ship lies in very deep water, in the open sea where currents can be powerful. The upper deck and the

smokestack (cut off to permit the passage of large ships) begin at over 98 ft (30 m) deep, while the stern and deck are between 170 ft (52 m) and 190 ft (58 m) deep. Visibility is usually good in the morning, but in the afternoon or if the water is murky, it's better to postpone your dive. All in all, if conditions are good, a dive on the *Haven* is one of the most exciting and thrilling experiences any scuba diver could have.

The wreck was colonized quickly and grew in an incredible manner, raising the curiosity of biologists. At first, there was an explosion of tube worms. Next, the dominant creatures were sea lilies, which covered the ship almost completely, making it seem as if every gallery, every cap-

82 top The base of the helm inside the bridge is now an empty box.

82 center and bottom The fire's high temperatures and long duration helped destroy the paints chrome plating and all of the ship's surface materials, permitting the spontaneous colonization of interesting forms of seabed life.

82-83 One of the roof hoists rises from the deep blue of the sea; the feather stars left, making room for other types of colonization.

83 top left and right All types of encrustations wrap around the oil tanker's instruments, including the electric controls for pumps and valves.

stan, every structure was cloaked in dense garlands of multicolored feathers.

Crinoids have diminished significantly over recent years, and in their place enormous quantities of colorful jewel anemones have appeared, along with sponges, oysters, sea squirts, alcyonarians, *Alicia mirabilis* anemones, and a real multitude of fish. These include incredible, dense clouds of swallowtail seaperch, schools of seabream, many exceptionally large scorpionfish, conger eels, mustelids, lobsters, mullets, and everything else — the entire gamut of Mediterranean fish.

Why such an incredible colonization in so short a time?

Biologists say it's quite simple: the *Haven* sank in a sandy area with strong currents and thus abundant plankton.

All around her is sand, with no reefs where sea creatures can attach themselves.

The fire cleaned the surface of the ship, practically sterilized her, thus permitting a rapid colonization by sea organisms, which found no obstacle, hindrance or counterindications. In fact, the pollution all around her made the wreck a choice area.

The size of the wreck and her

depth obviously require numerous dives for visitors to fully appreciate her extraordinary beauty.

Today, divers descend on one of the lines to the upper deck, less than 108 ft/33 m deep. You can stop in this large area to size up the situation. The first thing you'll note is the remains of the crosstree, with a hole from which a magnificent Conger eel peeps out. Clouds of swallowtail seaperch will immediately surround you, and you will see galleries decorated with magnificent jewel anemones.

Go on to the bridge below, which you can easily enter to see the base of

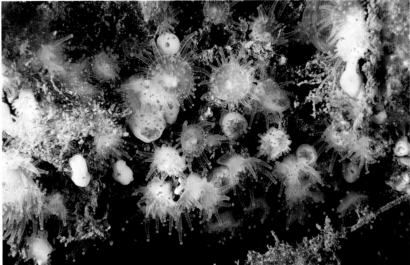

the helm and the electrical controls, behind which magnificent lobsters hide.

Then descend down the ladders, now decorated by oysters and more jewel anemones, to the lower decks, where you can enter the officers' cabins. Be careful, however, because the area is too small for many divers to enter at once. Continue on down to the rear quarterdeck.

All structures are completely colonized. There is something interesting wherever you look, so it's hard to decide whether to spend time looking at the details or admiring the imposing profile, galleries, the wings of the bridge (bent because of the fire), and ventilators.

One solution is to leave the deck and go up to the stern to admire the two soaring mast structures and the enormous smokestack, which has been cut off to allow you to examine the interior.

Another is to descend to the decks across from the bridge, where you can admire the capstans, mains, ladders and gangways.

From there, take a look up at the enormous bridge. Or look out from the galleries of the deck down to the ocean floor; it's so deep that it's impossible to see, even when the water is clear.

Real professionals might want to explore the "gash" (here the minimum depth is 155 ft (65 m) or even go down into the engine room. Note that it begins at 180 ft (55 m) and goes down to over 246 ft (75 m).

84 top A beautiful eel (Conger conger) found a hideout in a hole in the remains of a cross-toptree on the deck.

84-85 The rails of the various decks are covered by feather stars and crossed by red anthias. In the midst of the feather stars, a sea squirt (Phallusia mamillata) and many sea strands can be seen.

85 top left A veritable forest of feather stars chose the deck's frame as their home.

85 right The latest colonization on the Haven consists mainly of jewel anemones with very bright colors.

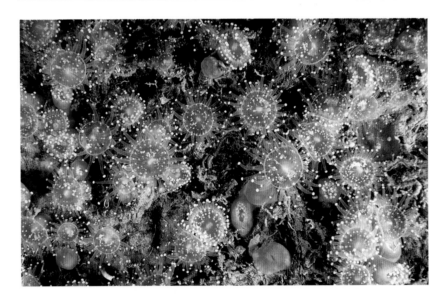

GENOVA

BY ALBERTO VANZO

Exploring the waters of Tigullio toward the east, you'll come to the wreck of the *Genova,* practically fated to be a victim of World War I. She was a large steamship built in Great Britain in 1904 at the Northumberland Shipbuilding Co. shipyard in Newcastle-upon-Tyne, and was launched under the name *Hillbrook.* She was 341 ft (104 m) long and had a gross tonnage of about 3500 tons. In 1913, the Angelo Parodi shipping company in Genoa purchased her; then in 1915, when war broke out, the Italian national railway requisitioned her to transport coal. Finally, in 1917, she was sold to Ilva Alti Forni.

The *Hillbrook*'s new owner had used her for only a few months when, on July 27, while she was en route to La Spezia with a load of artillery and other wartime matériel, a German submarine torpedoed her about 2 miles off Portofino. The torpedo hit her starboard side at the first fore hold. The commander nevertheless managed to reach Baia di Paraggi and moored at the diving platform, where the crew disembarked unharmed. The *Genova* floated for another eight hours, then slowly sank, sliding down bow first until she reached the sea floor about half a mile (900 m) from the coast. It was a long but avoidable agony as the ship, or at least her cargo, might have been saved had she been towed to the port of Santa Margherita or Rapallo. After the war, a Genoese company specializing in underwater work was hired to salvage the cargo. To do this, the divers had to completely uncover the holds. Thereafter, no one showed any further interest in the wreck, which local fishermen renamed *Il Vapore.*

86 top The Genova, a merchant ship that transported wartime materiel, sank during World War I in 1917, struck by a torpedo from a German U-Boat

86 bottom A school of swallowtail seaperch (Anthias anthias) who usually dwell on the wreck's stern rail

TECHNICAL CARD	
TYPE OF WRECK	Cargo ship
NATIONALITY	Italian
YEAR OF CONSTRUCTION	1904
DATE SUNK	July 27, 1917
CAUSE OF SINKING	Torpedoed
LOCATION	Between Castello di Paraggi and Portofino, Italy
DISTANCE FROM SHORE	2950 ft / 900 m
MINIMUM DEPTH	148 ft / 45 m
MAXIMUM DEPTH	250 ft / 61 m
LENGTH	341 ft / 104 m

148 ft / 45 m

250 ft / 61 m

88 The bow is an impressive sight; the top is 45 meters deep, and it is embedded in the mud at 61 meters deep.

89 top left The wreck has become more and more popular with divers over recent years, but this dive is only for divers with extensive experience in deep wrecks and conditions of poor visibility.

If you're lucky enough to dive onto the *Genova* on a day when visibility is ideal, a particularly magnificent sight will greet you. Even as you descend, following the lead line launched from the surface to the ship's deck, her size will become more and more impressive, reaching its apex as you approach the imposing bow, about 20 ft (6 m) high, which stands out perfectly upright in the deep blue sea. Do not descend to the sea floor here: it is 200 ft (61 m) deep and it would unduly shorten your dive. After a quick visit to the quarterdeck, as you swim over capstans, bollards, and various pieces of equipment on board, you'll come to the loading deck in the hold area. This area is not particularly interesting, but the hole that the torpedo created in the outer part of the hull is worth exploring. Going past two stairways located on the two sides of the loading deck, you'll come to the forecastle, where there is a very large number of fishing lines and nets among the remains of the bridge and cabins. Given the depth of the dive, this itinerary will have to end at the bridgehouse, after you examine the remains of the great smokestack. Another dive can be devoted to exploring the rest of the ship, where apart from the schools of sea perch, the stern is the most interesting sight. Take a look at the helm and the large, three-bladed propeller enveloped in a trawl net and cov-

ered with oysters.

In planning these dives, remember that they stretch the limits of recreational activity. Operating conditions make this a dive for experts who are experienced in diving on deep shipwrecks. In addition, remember that you should dive only when the sea is calm, using a well-known, proven surface organization. The wreck is in a location where maritime traffic is incessant, especially in the summer, and the

superfine silt on the sea floor often creates suspended particles that you cannot see from the surface but which are stratified in the deep water below. When we were making these dives for photographic purposes, there were times when we had to return regretfully to the surface as soon as we approached the wreck, because in this environment full of purchases, and hazards, the poor visibility would have made it extremely difficult for us to continue the dive.

89 top right This shows the fore loading deck toward the bridge and the area where the cabins were located; a bathtub remains in one of them on the right side of the ship.

89 bottom Nets and lines lost by fishermen who have frequented the wreck for over two generations are a constant danger during the entire dive; the photo shows the net wrapped around the starboard side of the bridge.

SESTRI KT

BY VINCENZO PAOLILLO

 pposite the promontory of Sestri Levante, about a mile offshore at the relatively challenging depth of 197 ft (60 m), is one of the most beautiful wrecks in the Mediterranean. Until two years ago, little was known about her. Some reports claimed she was a *Krieg Transporte,* or *KT*, a type of German war "war transport" that included many small units used for numerous tasks, including submarine destruction, as proved to be the case here.

We know that the vessel was sunk in late 1943. Some sources suggested she was of French origin: the engine-room telegraph bore the words *"avant"* and *"arrière."*

The true story emerged only recently, thanks to Claudio Corti and Marco Saibene's painstaking research in the Kriegsmarine's (German Navy's) historical registers.

Originally this mystery vessel was a truly magnificent yacht, built for Baron Henri de Rothschild in a French shipyard in 1926 and baptized *Eros*.

She was 213 ft (65 m) long and 32 ft (9.75 m) wide, with a displacement of 914 tons. The *Eros* had marvelous saloons and luxurious cabins and honorably fulfilled her duties as a floating *hôtel de luxe* until war broke out in 1939. The French Navy then requisitioned *Eros* and used her for diplomatic missions. At the end of 1939, however, she was equipped with light weapons, reclassified, and used to escort submarines and convoys along the Moroccan coast.

In 1942 the *Eros* returned to France. Renamed the *Incomprise,* she was assigned to patrol the French Mediterranean coast.

Then in late November, the Germans occupied Toulon and also took possession of the *Eros*. They used the Toulon shipyard to do major work on the ship and transform her into a U-Jäger — a submarine destroyer.

The afterdeck was completely exposed, the luminous saloons were eliminated, and an 88-mm cannon was installed, along with three platforms for anti-aircraft artillery and 8 underwater grenade launchers. On the foredeck, a 37-mm twin cannon was installed, and two 20-mm guns were positioned on each side, immediately fore and aft of the bridge. A

90 top The ship before her conversion for military use.

90 bottom Myriads of red anthias (Anthias anthias) swim in the partially gutted bridge.

TECHNICAL CARD

TYPE OF WRECK	Cargo ship
NATIONALITY	German
YEAR OF CONSTRUCTION	1926
DATE SUNK	September 14, 1944
CAUSE OF SINKING	Torpedoed
LOCATION	Between Punta Manara and Sestri Levante, Italy
DISTANCE FROM SHORE	about 1 mile / 1.6 km
MINIMUM DEPTH	115 ft / 35 m
MAXIMUM DEPTH	197 ft / 60 m
LENGTH	213 ft / 65 m

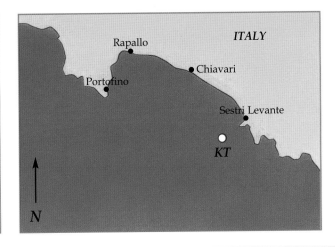

92 top A net is
caught on one of the
machine guns
located right behind
the deck.

92 bottom left
The forward cannon
is lit by divers and
surrounded by
anthias.

92 bottom right The
entrance of the hold
located near the stern
is now completely
encrusted.

93 The cloudy water
creates an aura of
mystery around the
KT's splendid bow.

sort of curious three-legged mast was installed on the bridge, apparently to be used as a terminal for listening equipment.

The ship, now renamed *U-J 2216,* reached her destination of Genoa in early 1944.

On 13 September 1944, she was assigned to escort two minelayers that were to create a new sea blockade near the port of La Spezia. Shortly before midnight, its mission complete, the little convoy began its return to Genoa, but was discovered by a passing Allied airplane (one of those that locals called Pippo), which launched flares and bombs, but did not hit the ships.

A few hours later, as she was approaching Sestri Levante at about 3.00 a.m., the *U.J.*'s listening devices picked up the noise of propellers. The captain gave the order to open fire, but owing to the looming darkness, no targets were identified or hit. The response was almost immediate. First a number of torpedoes passed very close to the *U-J 2216,* and at least one of them ended up on St. Anna beach, between Sestri Levante and Punta Manara. Then one struck the *U-J 2216*'s stern, which exploded with the munitions and antisubmarine grenades stored there, causing the vessel to sink within minutes.

Of the 95 crewmen on board, 57 were rescued by the minelayer and 9 by a small vedette that from Sestri Levante. Another 6 swam to shore, but 23 disappeared, with only 6 bodies recovered.

The dive is rather difficult. At 115 ft (35 m) down, the mast is the part of the ship closest to the surface, while the deck is between 174 ft (53 m) and 187 ft (57 m) below surface. Strong currents are not unusual, and often visibility is not the best, in which case you should postpone your dive. But if you're lucky enough to find clear water, this dive is absolutely fabulous.

At 115 ft (35 m), you will meet the tip of the curious three-legged mast-like structure, surrounded by incredible clouds of swallowtail sea perch (*Anthias anthias*). In their midst are large seabream, with silvery amberjacks darting by. Go to the roof of the bridgehouse, where a magnificent lobster lives peacefully. Before going to the bow, look around to the stern and admire the smokestack's curious profile.

Go to the deck and immediately, on a raised circular structure, you'll see the ship's light gun, still intact, in shooting position and completely encrusted with jewel anemones (*Corynactis viridis*). Swimming on, you'll come to the anchor capstans and then the splendid cutwater, with a strange shield right on top. Turn back to the bridgehouse: you can go in, but be careful of the many fishing lines and pieces of net lying about — they could easily ensnare you — and the unstable floor. The machine guns, also encrusted with jewel anemones, are located behind the bridgehouse, toward the smokestack.

It's easy to find large scorpionfish, cuttlefish, octopuses, and schools of seabream.

Just beyond, however, is where your visit should end: the stern, or what's left of it, is a mass of wreckage covered with very dangerous nets that could easily snare you owing in part to the fact that visibility is much poorer here. Currents raise the mud and envelop everything in an almost impenetrable cloud, even when the water is clear at the fore.

As you go back up, stop if you can for a moment at the top of the mast: when visibility is very good, the sight of the deck is truly exciting.

SESTRI ARMED CARGO SHIP

BY VINCENZO PAOLILLO

94 top During the work to recover the copper cargo, the central part of the ship was gutted, which is how it now appears to divers.

ITALY

Rapallo

Portofino

Chiavari

Sestri Levante

ARMED CARGO SHIP

N

98 ft / 30 m

118 ft / 36 m

95 bottom The photo shows the hoist on the bow roof. The tips of the anchor supports are still recognizable.

TECHNICAL CARD	
TYPE OF WRECK	*Cargo ship*
NATIONALITY	*German*
YEAR OF CONSTRUCTION	*Unknown*
DATE SUNK	*November, 1943*
CAUSE OF SINKING	*Enemy attack*
LOCATION	*Between Punta Manara and Sestri Levante, Italy*
DISTANCE FROM SHORE	*900 yds / 850 m*
MINIMUM DEPTH	*98 ft / 30 m*
MAXIMUM DEPTH	*118 ft / 36 m*
LENGTH	*262 ft / 80 m*

We know almost nothing about this wreck of a merchant ship, about 262 ft (80 m) long, with an estimated tonnage of 3000-4000 tons.

We do not know her name, her specifications, or the exact circumstances of her sinking. She was presumably a support ship for a German military convoy, equipped with light weapons to defend herself against possible attack. She had two medium-caliber cannons, one fore, the other aft, and at least 4 anti-aircraft machine guns on the long deck.

One day in November 1943, the ship, loaded with copper and munitions, was sailing along the coast to double the point at Sestri Levante when an Allied torpedo-bomber attack caught her by surprise. A torpedo struck the ship, causing a massive explosion that practically tore the vessel in two.

The exploding munitions in the ship's hold certainly added to effects of the hit, and she probably sank very quickly, in all likelihood carrying some of the crew with her.

Today she lies on the sea floor at a depth of from 118 ft (36 m) (at the bow) to 98 ft (30 m) (at the stern), broken in two but standing perfectly upright. The bow half faces out to sea, while the stern half, lying at a 45° angle to the bow section, is practically parallel to the coast.

The bow section is in rather good condition. The amidships section, destroyed by the explosion and postwar work by a salvage company that opened access to the two holds to salvage the cargo of copper, is now a formless mass of metal.

96 left This machine-gun carriage can be recognized on the roof of the armored hold.

96 right The ship's stately, majestic bow rises from the depths of Ligurian Sea.

Extremely dangerous nets now foul most of this section. The stern section is not in much better condition, although a little more of the structure remains, also covered by swathes of net.

You can start your diving from the bow, whose splendid, imposing cutwater rises perpendicular from the sea floor, offering what may be this wreck's very best photo opportunity. If you want to explore the stern section, you should do it in a separate dive.

It's not a deep dive, but there are some distances to travel. For some odd reason visibility on the stern section is much worse than on the fore section, where it is usually good.

On the afterdeck, you can see what remains of the cannon bed, with various large artillery shells and a complicated but still well-preserved system of capstans and pulleys, with swallowtail seaperch, pickerels and small schools of seabream swimming in their midst.

A portion of the deck on the starboard side has come apart owing to corrosion, and you can see the interior of the hull.

SESTRI ARMED CARGO SHIP

97 top left Part of the original charge can still be found inside the hold.

97 top center An octopus peeps out between the roof's metal sheets.

97 top right Colonies of yellow anemones (Corynactis viridis) embellish the wreck's frame.

97 bottom Over the years many fishing nets have snagged on the hoists and bollards.

A lovely, extremely curious octopus has built its den beneath the wreckage of the deck. It loves to play with divers.

From the forecastle, go down the long bridge using the two ladders. At their midpoint is one of the openings to the inside.

On the deck are the machine-gun beds with the cranks still in good condition, some draped with pieces of net. The arms, on the other hand, have probably ended up in the homes of collectors. Several large projectiles and semi-circular cartridge clips are still perfectly visible. Beautiful colonies of jewel anemones *(Corynactis viridis)* have covered the galleries.

But what you should examine carefully is the floor of the deck. Here you'll find a true festival of nudibranchs *(Flabellina affinis, Hypselodoris tricolor, Cratena peregrina,* and more), dotted sea slugs *(Peltodoris atromaculata)*, hermit crabs, and Galatea crabs.

You can enter the ship either from a porthole in the center of the deck or through the gash caused by the explosion, but there is not much to see — everything that was once there has been carried off. Before coming back up, take a good look around in the sand, where you can see many projectiles, and then be sure to look up: the usual visitors to this wreck are amberjacks *(Seriola dumerili)*, with a profusion of ocean sunfish *(Mola mola)*.

B-17 E

BY ROBERTO RINALDI

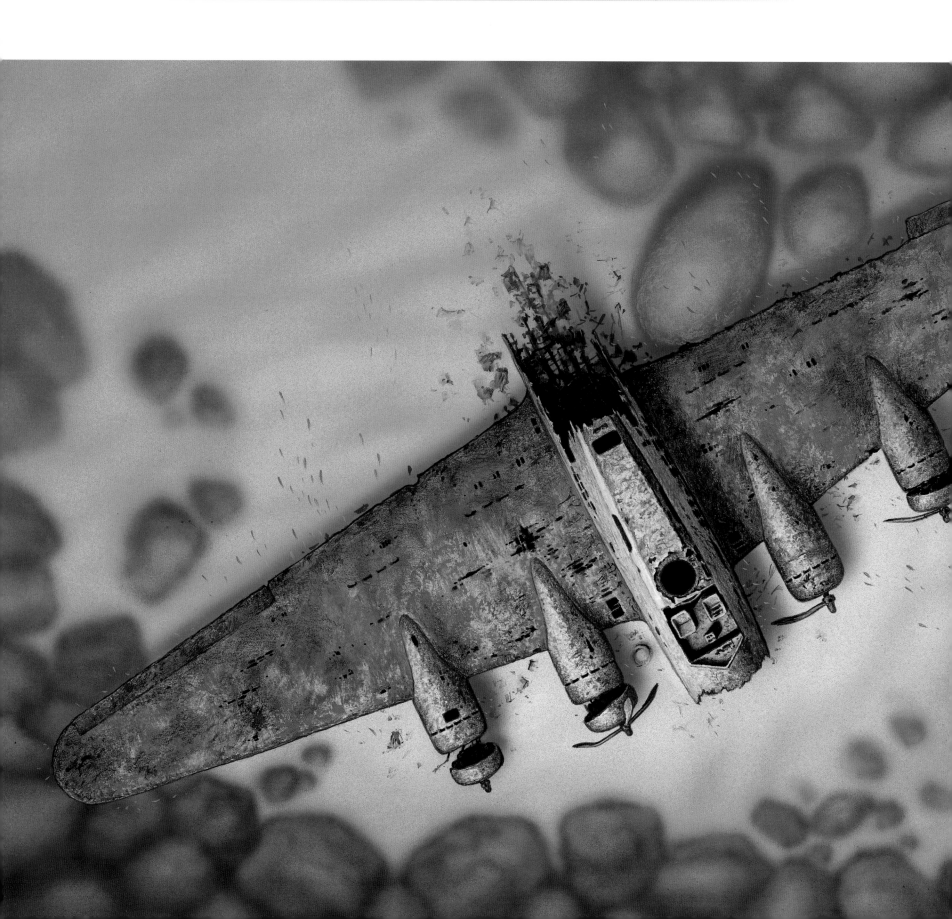

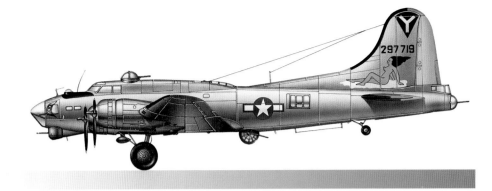

TECHNICAL CARD

TYPE OF WRECK	Bomber
NATIONALITY	American
YEAR OF CONSTRUCTION	Unknown
DATE SUNK	February 14, 1944
CAUSE OF SINKING	Damaged during a mission
LOCATION	Calvi, Corsica
DISTANCE FROM SHORE	656 ft / 200 m
MINIMUM DEPTH	75 ft / 23 m
MAXIMUM DEPTH	88 ft / 27 m
LENGTH	75 ft / 23 m

SAN FRANCISCO
POINT

N

B-17 E
• Cittadella

Calvi

CORSICA

75 ft / 23 m
88 ft / 27 m

I t's a singular experience to find an airplane on the sea floor. Such wrecks are rare and certainly fascinating, especially when, as in this case, the plane crash is part of an adventure story.

The old plane that now lies in 82 ft (25 m) of water across from the citadel of Calvi has an exciting tale to tell. First of all, it was a famous type of aircraft, one that flew the skies during World War II. The *B-17* was a Boeing model, a bomber whose size and formidable weapons gave it the nickname of "Flying Fortress." It was in fact armed with 13 machine guns, could carry eight tons of bombs, and had a flying range of 2000 miles (3220 km). And this aircraft had come from far away when it sank in the waters off Corsica. It had left a base in southern Italy to bomb the Verona railroad junction. It was February 14, 1944. The pilot's name was Frank Chaplick, and he was part of an attack unit comprised of dozens of Flying Fortresses escorted by a number of fighter squadrons.

But during the attack, Chaplick's *B-17* became isolated, and was then attacked by a German fighter. It was struck in various areas, and some crew members were injured or killed. Soon the *B-17* was no longer able to defend itself, as its gunners were either injured or dead. The turrets were damaged, one engine was dead and another was damaged. Nothing remained but escape.

Chaplick decided to aim for Corsica, where he could land at Calvi airport. After a dramatic, perilous

99 bottom A diver swims along the plane's fuselage, being careful not to raise sediment that would make the water cloudy.

98 top and 99 top The B-17 was the most powerful bomber of those used by Americans during World War II. It had a carrying capacity of 16,000 lbs / 7200 kg and a 1860 mile / 3000 km range.

99 center A B-17 photographed mid-mission. The frame of the nose can be seen in which the machine gun caps are discerniable. They have disappeared from aircraft sunk near Calvi.

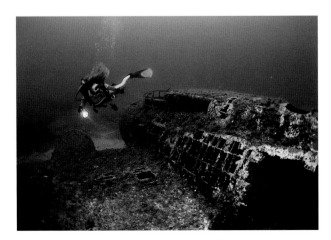

*100 top
The starboard
propeller still has its
three blades. The fact
that they are bent
indicates that the
propeller was still
turning when the
plane hit the water.*

*It is likely that this
was the only engine
functioning at the
time of the accident.
The internal engine
compartments now
make excellent
hiding places for
young fish.*

*100 bottom The
right wing tip of the
B-17 wreck has a
multitude of
madreporic
encrustations.
A school of snappers
is hidden under the
other wing.*

*100-101 A diver
swims vertically
along the cockpit
that housed the
machine gun. Two
of the 13 light guns
that armed the B-17
were located behind
the pilot.*

flight, he immediately realized that the landing strip was too short for his *B-17,* particularly given its damaged condition. After a couple of attempts, he decided to make a water landing. So, after unloading his last remaining munitions, Chaplick slowly descended and tipped the tail of the *B-17* in the water, pulling it off from the rest of the plane. The landing was successful and the six crew members had two minutes to get out before the *B-17* vanished permanently beneath the waves.

The plane is still there today, intact and impressive. With a wingspan of 98 ft (30 m), it is clearly visible in the crystalline waters as it lies on the sea floor. Some propeller blades are missing, except for those on the first starboard engine, which still has all three, twisted and contorted by the impact with the water. The aircraft's nose section is quite damaged, while the cockpit is still extremely interesting, as the pilots' seats and some of the controls are in place.

It is possible to enter the plane

from the back, as well as the gunner's upper turret, now missing the cup and machine gun. Numerous encrusting sponges have colonized the plane, and now cover it almost completely. Divers may also see large crabs and swarms of small seabream, which take shelter in the Poseidon grass on the seabed as divers approach.

Owing to its technical simplicity, a visit to the wreck of the Calvi *B-17* is highly recommended to anyone with a passion for the sea and its tragic tales.

101 top The pilots' seats and controls are still clearly visible. Here, as in all internal parts of the airplane, schools of fish abound.

VICKERS VIKING

BY ALBERTO VANZO

I t's not easy to find this wreck, which lies on a sandy sea floor full of Neptune grass in an inlet without any particular landmarks. And even if you use a sonic depth finder, it becomes difficult to distinguish the signal owing to the minimum bathymetric range between the bottom and the most prominent point of the fuselage. A good search system is to drag a free diver behind the boat, an operation that often requires time and some physical effort. You should begin the search by concentrating on the area closest to the north side of the bay, at a bathymeter reading between 36 ft (11 m) and 43 ft (13 m), proceeding at moderate speed and trying to traverse the area using land references.

With a great deal of patience, the shallow depth and visibility of the water will help identify the wreck, and any effort and energy you

TECHNICAL CARD	
TYPE OF WRECK	Passenger aircraft
NATIONALITY	British
YEAR OF CONSTRUCTION	Unknown
DATE SUNK	Unknown
CAUSE OF SINKING	Water landing – engine failure
LOCATION	Mortoli Bay, Corsica
DISTANCE FROM SHORE	656 ft / 200 m
MINIMUM DEPTH	36 ft / 11 m
MAXIMUM DEPTH	43 ft / 13 m
LENGTH	66 ft / 20 m

expend will certainly be repaid by this beautiful, easy dive.

This Vickers' twin-engine plane, which was leased by the Holiday on Ice ice-skating troupe in the 1950s, was flying over Corsica when it had an engine breakdown and began to lose altitude. The pilot, who did not think he could reach the nearest airport, was forced to try a landing over Mortoli Bay, and because the beach was full of rocky formations,

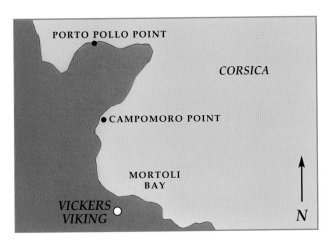

PORTO POLLO POINT

CORSICA

CAMPOMORO POINT

MORTOLI BAY

VICKERS VIKING

N

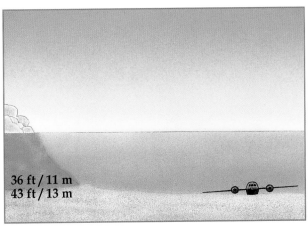

36 ft / 11 m
43 ft / 13 m

*102 top The design
of the* Vickers
Viking, *begun in
1946 and intended
for passenger
transport, came from
the famous
Wellington bomber.
More than 160
models were made
and kept in service
into the end of the
1950s.*

*102 bottom
The most
enchanting view of
the plane is from the
front of the pilots'
cabin, slightly to
one side, from which
its good state of
preservation can be
appreciated.*

he decided to make a water landing. His skill, and perhaps the good physical condition of the passengers on board, helped avert a tragedy, and everyone survived by swimming to shore. Upon impact with the water, the fuselage cracked, and the plane sank without the tail section.

Although over the years trophy hunters have carried off everything it was possible to take (including the propeller blades), the plane's fuselage and wings are still relatively intact

and completely safe. This dive will thus satisfy the most demanding enthusiast, and at the same time is an excellent training ground for less expert divers who are trying out a sunken wreck for the first time. Because of the transparent water, which allows you to see the form of the plane from the surface when the sea is calm, you can reach the airplane even by free diving. If you use a tank, the relatively shallow depth and usually gentle current within the

105 top left Because of the missing hatch cover, the large tire, still in its compartment, can be seen on the left wing.

105 top right The propeller blades of the two Bristol Hercules 634 engines were not lost on the impact but unfortunately were removed.

105 center Wires and aluminum scraps are spread throughout the inside of the cockpit.

105 bottom All of the chairs and onboard controls were removed from the pilots' cabin and cockpit.

104-105 The plane, a twin-engined Vickers, carried a troupe of ice skaters from Holiday on Ice in the 1950s. Engine failure forced it to make a water landing in the Bay of Mortoli.

104 bottom Upon impact with the water, the body split and the tip was completely lost. The rest of the airplane can be entered from this point of the cockpit.

inlet make it possible to explore the wreck in detail. The best way to start this dive is to swim just below the water's surface to get an overall view of the plane. The best view will be from the cockpit, which is slightly off to the side, giving you the feeling that the plane is flying at you.

The wings with their powerful Bristol Hercules 1690-hp radial engines, are intact, and you can see the landing gear, still closed because it was not used during the descent. You can enter the airplane from the broken part of the fuselage. Cables and aluminum wreckage are scattered everywhere, and it's hard to imagine that you're inside an elegant, albeit a bit dated, airborne living-room of the past. The torch lights revive the colors of the marine encrustation that has colonized the wreckage. Soft light enters from the outside, through the openings where the portholes once existed in the cockpit and passenger areas, allowing you to explore even without using artificial light.

KT 12

BY EGIDIO TRAINITO

TECHNICAL CARD	
TYPE OF WRECK	Armed military cargo ship
NATIONALITY	German
YEAR OF CONSTRUCTION	1943
DATE SUNK	June 10, 1943
CAUSE OF SINKING	Torpedoed by a submarine
LOCATION	Orosei Bay, Sardinia
DISTANCE FROM SHORE	2 miles / 3.2 km
MINIMUM DEPTH	79 ft / 24 m
MAXIMUM DEPTH	112 ft / 34 m
LENGTH	About 250 ft / 60 m

The *KT 12* and its twin unit the *KT 11* were designed by Deutsche Werft of Hamburg and built at the OTO works in Livorno, Italy for the German Kriegsmarine.

The *KT 12* was an armed military cargo ship used to transport provisions, motor vehicles, and fuel to North Africa.

She was delivered on May 19, 1943 and on June 10, during her maiden voyage, she was attacked by the British submarine *Safari*, about 2 miles (3.2 km) off the eastern coast of Sardinia, near the Orosei Marina.

The *Safari* fired three torpedoes. One hit, striking the *KT 12*'s bow, breaking it right off. This section sank immediately, while the ship, beset by a raging fire, listed for 41 minutes before she too sank.

Of her 53 officers and men, only 3

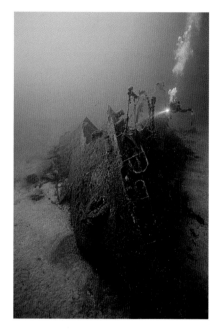

survived. Even today, eyewitnesses recall the bodies of the sailors who made it to land still alive but terribly burned.

Some inhabitants of Orosei still call the *KT 12* "the oil tanker," because long after the ship sank, barrels of fuel continued to float to the surface. Many were recovered from the sea floor, and the gasoline they contained was used to power tractors and every other type of engine.

To make a complete exploration of the *KT 12*, you'll need at least 3 dives, one to the hull, one to the bow section, and one to the truck section. The sea floor is always sandy and the depth never exceeds 112 ft (34 m), while visibility is often optimal owing to practically ever-present current.

The hull is upright and the shallowest part is 79 ft (24 m) deep. Your dive will usually start from the stern, where the propellers are clearly visible.

Going up to the bow, you'll see the helm, and on the upper deck a 75-mm cannon, with its muzzle pointed upward, facing the stern.

106 top The bow section, sliced off by the torpedo explosion, lies on the sea floor about 2625 ft (800 m) from the hull. The anchors are still in the hawseholes and parts of the nets are still entangled in the wreckage.

106 bottom The KT 12 is shown sailing during a trial run before being delivered to the German navy. Built in the OTO works of Livorno, on June 10, 1943, during her first voyage to Africa, the ship was sunk by the British submarine the Safari.

79 ft / 24 m

112 ft / 34 m

Farther ahead is the skylight with a smokestack. Of the two machine guns that were on the sides, one has fallen to the starboard side of the ship, while the support for the port side one is still standing, with the muzzle lying on the deck.

On the port side, the lifeboat davits are still in place. Farther on, the cabin area, where the bulkheads are almost completely corroded, leads to the engine room.

An anchor on a long chain abandoned by a large ship has destroyed the command room. Just beyond is the great fore hold, where there are still numerous barrels of fuel, and often you will see a fine group of seabream. On deck, a pair of derricks and various capstans separate the hold from the torpedo's zone of impact, with its contorted wreckage.

Along the starboard side of the ship, among masses of metal, barrels and various pieces of equipment, are two hoists, with rubber wheels lying on one side.

The bow is lying on the port side, with the uppermost part 85 ft (26 m) from the surface, and is about 2625 ft (800 m) from the hull.

The two Hall anchors are still in the hawseholes, while in the upper portion there is a tangle of nets.

On the deck fragment, which is almost vertical, there are bollards, capstans, and munitions cases. Inside,

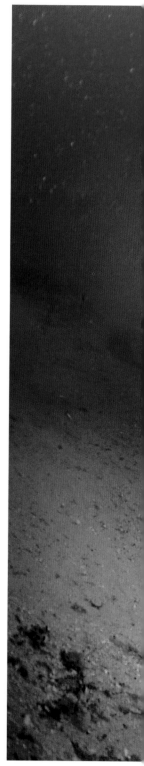

108 top The gun mounted on the quarterdeck is completely covered with sponges and algae.

108 center The ship's helm can still be seen on the quarterdeck, but has lost its wooden portions.

108 bottom This anchor was used as a spare, or "life-saver."

108-109 The action of currents on the sea floor has produced a depression near the rudder and the two propellers.

109 top left The truck had twin back wheels for better loading capacity. The front wheels are turned, probably as a result of the impact with the seabed.

you'll see dozens of large bream, a cloud of banded blacktails, white seabream and many sea eels.

A little over 165ft/50 m from the bow is a large mass of cargo parts that were lost while the hull was listing.

There is a chassis from a heavy transport truck, with its font wheels with their rubber tires turned and with double back wheels and tires. The engine and steering column are clearly visible, but there are no remains of the body.

Nearby is a trolley with a power unit or large pump.

All around are the remains of a large number of fuel barrels, most of which have collapsed.

A large brown grouper is always circling among the trucks and other remains.

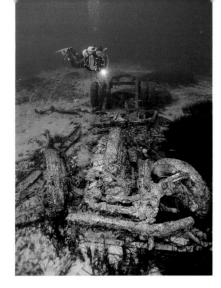

109 top right The KT 12's square-shaped stern is covered with equipment that is difficult to identify. A gun is visible on the upper part of the forecastle.

KT 12

LST

BY ROBERTO RINALDI

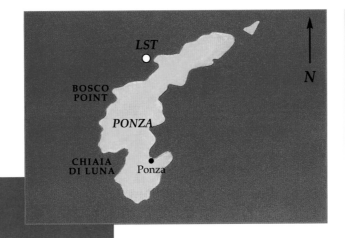

T
he sinking of an *LST* in the waters off Ponza was truly dramatic, a drama within the drama of World War II.

LST stands for Landing Ship Tank, a type of craft designed for action in the Mediterranean, when the Axis forces were still masters of the ports and the only way the Allies could make a landing was to attack a stretch of coast or beach. The *LSTs* were developed for just this purpose. Over 328 ft (100 m) long, they had a negligible draft and were thus capable of sailing right up on to the beach, where they could lower the ports and permit men and machinery to disembark. *LSTs* were not meant for general navigation or traversing rough seas.

This is the drama of an *LST* en route from Anzio to Naples during the night of February 22-23, 1943.

In addition to the crew, the *LST* carried various provisions, two small tanks, and 50 German prisoners.

TECHNICAL CARD

TYPE OF WRECK	*Landing vessel*
NATIONALITY	*English*
YEAR OF CONSTRUCTION	*1942*
DATE SUNK	*February 23, 1943*
CAUSE OF SINKING	*Storm*
LOCATION	*Punta Papa, Ponza, Italy*
DISTANCE FROM SHORE	*324 ft / 100 m*
MINIMUM DEPTH	*59 ft / 18 m*
MAXIMUM DEPTH	*85 ft / 26 m*
LENGTH	*262 ft / 80 m divided into 2 sections*

110 top The wreck lies on the sandy seabed. The Allied landing ship transport still seems to be sailing, with the bow door ready to land men and vehicles; its machine guns are pointed forward.

111 bottom Men and tanks inside the ship once waited for the door to lower, when they would be greeted by enemy gunfire

as they landed on the beach.
Today, spectacular patterns of light create an extremely evocative environment.

The raging storm that had struck this stretch of sea forced the skipper to seek refuge west of Ponza.

But the cumbersome craft struggled with the waves and wind and was hard to control. In addition, one of the two engines failed, greatly worsening the navigational situation.

Soon the *LST* began to crash against the reefs, and all on board abandoned the vessel. Residents of Ponza came to the rescue, throwing floating ropes into the water. Later in the night, a great explosion broke the vessel in two.

Despite rescue efforts, casualties were extremely heavy, and only 30 of the sailors, soldiers, and prisoners were saved.

The captain killed himself with a pistol shot to the head.

None of this drama is evident in the dive, which is pleasant and very easy, on a sea floor that never exceeds a depth of 82 ft (25 m). In such clear water that you can see the ship from the surface without even using a mask. In all, the area around the wreck is easy to traverse, given the excellent visibility and shallow depth.

There are two sections to visit, lying about 324 ft (100 m) from each other. The bow section is what attracts most scuba divers.

It is famous primarily for its anti-aircraft gun and machine guns still balanced on their support after sixty years under salt water.

The forward section lies upright about 324 ft (100 m) from the rocks off Punta Papa.

The bow is open, as the doors that permitted troops to land were destroyed as the ship sank.

There is a large tunnel under the deck that you can easily go through.

Some parts of the walls are covered with colonies of yellow gorgonians, while the patterns of sunlight that filter in through the openings of the bridge make the environment highly evocative.

As you go through the ship's interior, don't miss the bridge, and be sure to take photos near the forward machine guns or the light cannon. To find the after section, swim toward the sea floor into the beautiful bay. The stern is also lying upright, but the hull is covered with much more sand than the bow section.

The stern is less spectacular, although it has one completely intact cabin and several capstans that make good photographs.

112-113 To the fore, the machine guns and turret with its cannon make a fabulous photo.

113 top You can easily enter this vast area, where you'll be able to admire the little branches of yellow gorgonians that thrive in the current.

LST

LAURA C

BY ROBERTO RINALDI

Don Ferdinando, a former diver in the Italian Navy, was born in Licata, Sicily. He was assigned to salvage the cargo of the *Laura C,* an Italian merchant ship torpedoed and sunk off Capo dell'Armi.

In summer 1941 the *Laura C* completed loading in Trieste. She was to deliver her cargo within six months, as needed, to Axis troops fighting in Africa.

This cargo included explosives, spare parts, telephone lines, bottles of beer and wine, and other materials. When the *Laura C* left the Adriatic, she was supposed to head to Messina to join a convoy that would be escorted to its destination.

But while crossing the straits, she was attacked and torpedoed by a British submarine.

The charge killed one man in the engine room and seriously damaged the helm.

Attempts were made to tow the vessel and strand her, but it was too

late: although the bow was resting on the sandy bottom, the stern sank beneath the water.

To make matters worse, the *Laura C* had foundered right at the mouth of a river, which slowly pushed her along the muddy slope and pulled her under.

Here at the wreck site, Don Ferdinando's adventures began.

Wearing heavy shoes, a copper helmet and a rubberized suit, and protected from the cold by layers of

114 top Above the great holds are the capstans serving cargo booms used in loading goods.

114 bottom The Laura C, *shown here in a period photo, had left Trieste bound for Messina when she was attacked and sunk off Capo dell'Armi.*

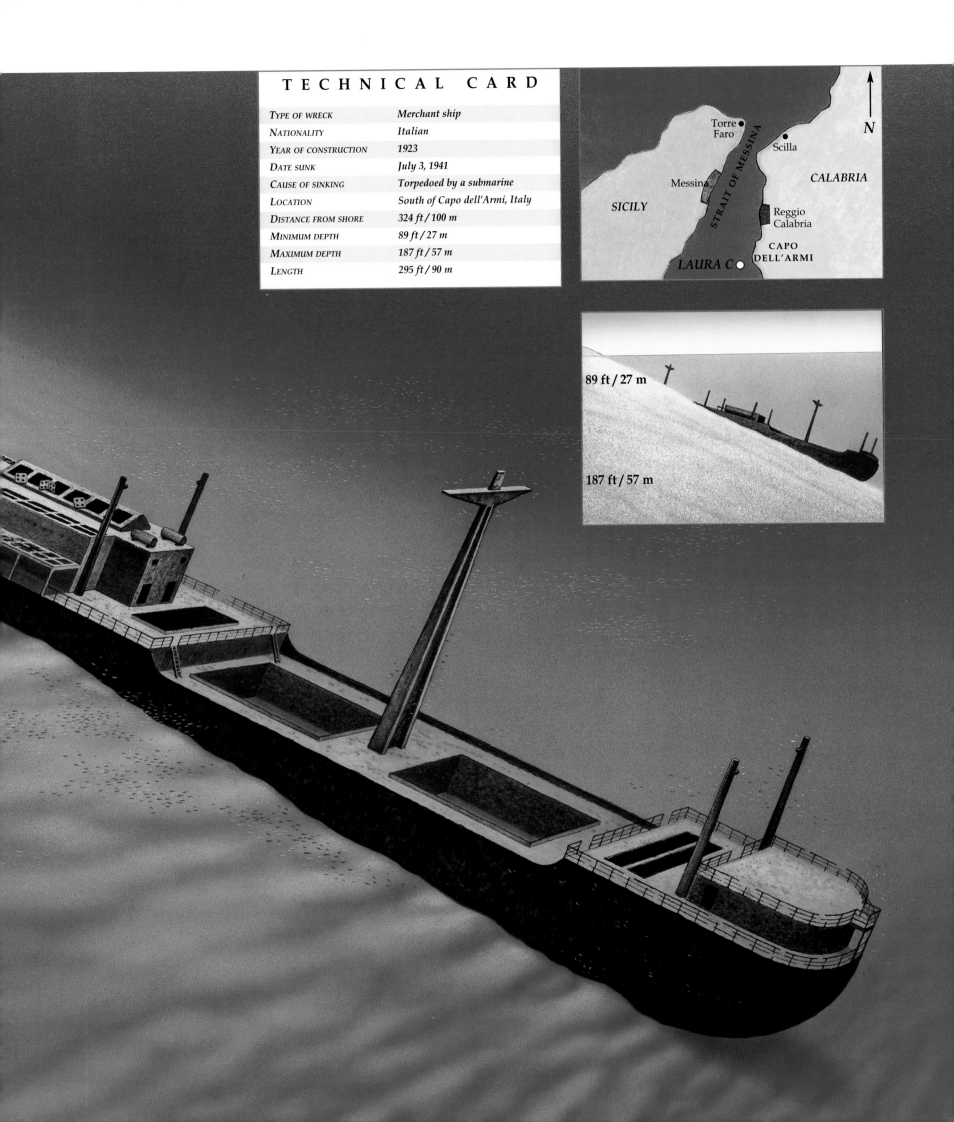

TECHNICAL CARD

TYPE OF WRECK	Merchant ship
NATIONALITY	Italian
YEAR OF CONSTRUCTION	1923
DATE SUNK	July 3, 1941
CAUSE OF SINKING	Torpedoed by a submarine
LOCATION	South of Capo dell'Armi, Italy
DISTANCE FROM SHORE	324 ft / 100 m
MINIMUM DEPTH	89 ft / 27 m
MAXIMUM DEPTH	187 ft / 57 m
LENGTH	295 ft / 90 m

N

Torre
Faro

Scilla

Messina

CALABRIA

SICILY

STRAIT OF MESSINA

Reggio
Calabria

CAPO
DELL'ARMI

LAURA C

89 ft / 27 m

187 ft / 57 m

sweaters, he gradually salvaged the cargo, working in the ship for two years. Meanwhile, men on the salvage boat hand-pumped air into the hose by maneuvering the oars. Cases of wine and beer came up to the surface. Bottles of Campari. Reels of electrical wire, car parts. And large quantities of explosives.

"I can do anything I want with the dynamite," bragged Don Ferdi-nando. "When the water is too murky in a hold, I can place one charge on one side and another on the other and blast open two holes so the current can get in to cleanse the water."

And after almost sixty years of oblivion, those very explosives were what brought the ship back into the news. In fact, rumor had it that the TNT used for some of the Mafia's most atrocious crimes came from here. So the ship was sequestered for several years. Finally, in 2002, the holds were sealed with cement, thus permanently closing the book on the mysterious cargo of the *Laura C.*

Now it is once again possible to visit the remains of the wreck.

Jump in from the shore and follow the sandy plateau, until you see a mast poking up out of the mud.

The bow now lies in the muddy bottom along with cargo holds nos. 1 and 2, once full of cases of Chianti and Dreher beer.

The first good structure that appears is the skylight in the engine room, which can be traversed without great difficulty.

The engine room is large and worth exploring.

Going on toward the stern, you'll

116 top Going aft, you'll find the soaring mast that was used to support the cargo booms. Today the mast is richly encrusted with seabed life, and surrounded by a cloud of damselfish and chromids.

116 bottom
A diver explores the
engine-room
skylights, which are
covered with
encrustations but
are still in good
condition.

116-117 A capstan
rises behind the
bunk structures
near no. 3 hold,
the only one visible, as
the first and second
ones are buried
beneath sediment.

LAURA C

see the remains of bunks, and some
of the furniture is still visible. If you
look carefully, you'll see a number of
fish, including rather large groupers
and many wreckfish, especially in the
open sea, near the large mast that still
rises to the surface, surrounded by a
dense school of anthias.

The cabins face the holds. Once
glass bottleheads poked out of the
mud here, along with vials of per-
fume and a large number of inkpots.
In the next hold, at a depth of 164 ft
(50 m), there were bottles of Campari.
And here, according to Don Ferdi-
nando, the ship carried 1325 lbs (600
kg) of explosives.

Today, both holds remain sealed
with cement. The after section is very
beautiful, framed by elegant shrouds
and rigging and enlivened by a number of structures still in excellent condition. The propeller also makes an
impressive visit. But we're now at a
depth of about 184 ft (56 m).

117 top left This hold
contains the remains
of the little bottles of
Campari that were its
cargo. It is said that
the explosive was
hidden here.

117 center right
It is quite easy and
safe to enter the
engine room, given
the large openings
and areas.

117 bottom
The bulwarks, rails,
and ladders have been
colonized by algae
and microorganisms
but are still in good
condition.

RED SEA AND

BY EGIDIO TRAINITO

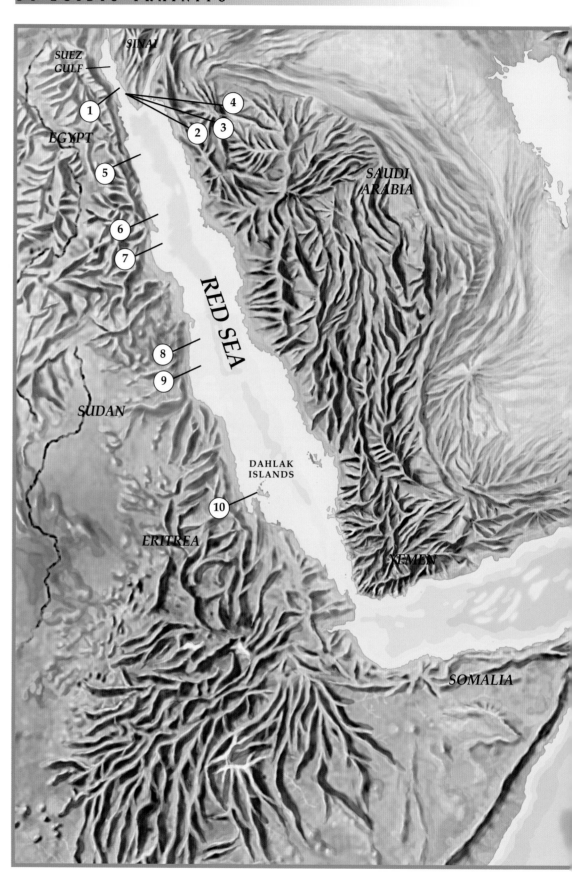

The Indian Ocean is the smallest of the planet's three great oceans. Although the Red Sea accounts for only a small portion of it (just 0.6%), since November 17, 1869, when the Suez Canal opened, the Red Sea has been its nerve center for naval traffic between East and West. Suffice it to note that each year about 14,000 large-tonnage ships traverse the canal to sail down the Red Sea. And it's a sea fraught with danger: numerous projecting reefs, winds that can be impetuous, and powerful currents that sweep through the narrow passages among the coral reefs. Not unnaturally, most of the known wrecks in the Indian Ocean are in the Red Sea.

About 30 wrecks along the coasts of Egypt, Sudan and Eritrea, on the Red Sea's western coast, attract frequent visits by diving center boats and scuba charters. A cluster of wrecks can be found in the Straits of Gubal, where the *Thistlegorm,* one of the world's most famous wrecks, now lies. While this British ship was the victim of war, many ships have foundered in peacetime on the emerging reefs that dot the mandatory point of passage through the straits. Of these, Sha'ab Abu Nuhas Reef has claimed the most victims. There are at least 4 shipwrecks along its shores, the remains of ships that went off course and foundered here. These are some of the most popular shipwrecks in the entire Red Sea, and information about three of them is provided in this volume.

World War II caused the loss of many other ships in the Red Sea. These were primarily Italian ships stationed in the ports and bays of what was then Italian East Africa. When Italy entered the war in 1941, the order was to scuttle the ships, thereby rendering them useless to the Allied forces. However, the

INDIAN OCEAN

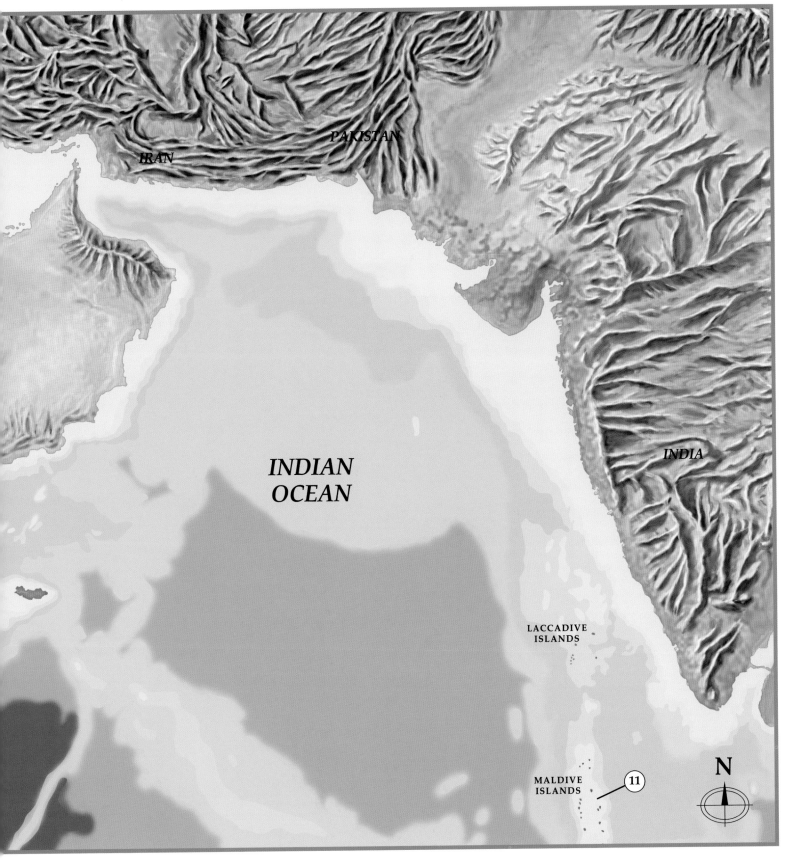

IRAN

PAKISTAN

INDIA

INDIAN
OCEAN

LACCADIVE
ISLANDS

MALDIVE
ISLANDS — 11

N

1) THISTLEGORM

2) GHIANNIS D

3) CARNATIC

4) CHRISOULA K.

5) NUMIDIA

6) TUGBOAT

7) CARGO SHIP

8) BLUE BELT

9) UMBRIA

10) NAZARIO SAURO

11) "SHIPYARD"

INDIAN OCEAN

British salvaged and reused many of them, while others have remained at the bottom of the sea floor, their cargoes intact. This was the case of the wrecks near the Dahlak Islands in Eritrea, and in particular that of the *Umbria*, which was scuttled off Wingate Reef, across from Port Sudan. Owing to the shallow depth and the rich cargo (which is still almost completely intact), the *Umbria* is one of the most fascinating wrecks known.

Dives on Red Sea wrecks enjoy especially favorable conditions. The water is clear and warm (even in the winter the temperature never drops below 20° C/ 68° F), and there are extensive tourist structures, making it possible to organize thematic cruises that almost always include visits to wrecks. In addition, there is an extraordinary proliferation of organisms covering the submerged wreckage, in particular filter

120-121 A diver illuminates the masts of the Ghiannis D., *which sank on Abu Nuhas Reef in the Straits of Gubal in the Red Sea*

121 The metallic structure of the Ghiannis D. *is completely covered with alcyonarians and colorful corals: shipwrecks always offer materials that can support hanging life forms.*

feeders, which are nevertheless an indication of how often the current is a factor in diving on these wrecks.

Compared to the concentration of wrecks in the Red Sea, there are few easily accessible wrecks in other areas of the Indian Ocean. In the Maldives, for instance, there are only about 10 such wrecks. This is probably due to a number of factors: the principal commercial routes are far from land, and many areas are not open to underwater tourism, both along the coast of East Africa and on the Indian Sea's other shores.

THISTLEGORM

BY CLAUDIO CANGINI

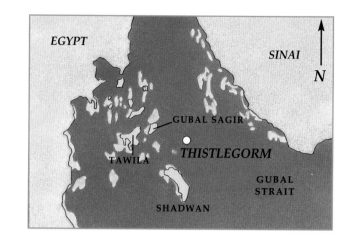

The *Thistlegorm* (Gaelic for "Blue Thistle") was built by the Joseph L. Thompson & Sons, Sunderland, Great Britain, and launched on 9 April 1940. She was a cargo ship owned by the Albyn Line Ltd.

Her coal boilers generated almost 2000 horsepower, harnessed by a three-cylinder engine driving a propeller that gave her a cruising speed of over 10 knots.

She was over 426 ft (130 m) long and 59 ft (18 m) wide and displaced over 9000 tons. During the war, the Royal Navy requisitioned her, primarily to transport foodstuffs from the Americas.

For defense, the *Thistlegorm* had a cannon and two machine guns, one heavy, the other a turret-mounted anti-aircraft gun. In September 1941, the *Thistlegorm* sailed from Glasgow on her fourth mission — transporting military matériel for the British Eighth Army in North Africa, where operations were to include the launching of a heavy attack on Rommel's troops.

The *Thistlegorm*'s holds and decks carried Jeeps and Morris automobiles, Bedford heavy vehicles, trucks loaded with BSA and Norton motorcycles, two tanks, two locomotives with their cars, airplane wings, cases of Lee-Enfield rifles, a large arsenal of explosives, and boots and uniforms for the troops. Her destination was Alexandria, Egypt, but the Mediterranean Sea was controlled by Italian and German naval forces and patrolled by deadly U-boats. To make the mission less risky, the British General Staff decided the ship should reach Suez by circumnavigating Africa.

TECHNICAL CARD	
TYPE OF WRECK	Armed cargo ship
NATIONALITY	English
YEAR OF CONSTRUCTION	1940
DATE SUNK	October 6, 1941
CAUSE OF SINKING	Bombing raid
LOCATION	Gubal Strait, Egypt
DISTANCE FROM SHORE	About 8 miles / 13 km
MINIMUM DEPTH	46 ft / 14 m
MAXIMUM DEPTH	105 ft / 32 m
LENGTH	446 ft / 136 m

When the *Thistlegorm* entered the Gubal Strait near Sha'ab Ali, she found other Allied ships anchored and waiting for the Suez Canal to be freed from mines and a cleared of a vessel that had sunk on the Mediterranean side. The *Thistlegorm* was ordered to anchor.

On the night of 5-6 October 1941 a squadron of long-range Heinkel HE-111German bombers, based in Crete, sighted the convoy and began bombing. Two bombs hit no. 4 hold and triggered a chain reaction explosion that ripped the stern section, causing the *Thistlegorm* to sink. She had 49 persons on board; of them 9 crewmen, 5 gunners, and 4 sailors lost their lives.

122 bottom The photograph shows various discoveries from the wreck: dishes, bottles of beer, a faucet and a number of portholes.

123 top right The English shipyard Joseph L. Thompson & Sons Ltd. launched the Thistlegorm *on April 9, 1940 from Sunderland. When sunk only 18 months later, she was on her fourth mission.*

46 ft / 14 m

105 ft / 32 m

124 top The after section, separated from the rest of the ship, is resting on its port side on the sea floor. The Thistlegorm's weapons can still be seen on the forecastle: a heavy mobile machine gun and a 4-inch cannon.

124 bottom left The entire bow section of the Thistlegorm is in excellent condition.

124 bottom right One of the two anchors is visible on the bow bulwark, as the captain had lowered only one anchor before the ship sank.

THISTLEGORM

This was the tragic last act in the brief life of this famous Royal Navy cargo ship.

The wreck of the *Thistlegorm* is southeast of Sha'ab Ali, a group of coral formations alternating with shallow lagoons 10 miles (16 km) long and 3 miles (4.8 km) wide at the southern entry to the Gulf of Suez. The hull, which sank upright, is resting with its keel on a sandy-detrital seabed about 105 ft (32 m) deep, with the bow facing northwest and the superstructures 46 ft (14 m) from the surface.

The *Thistlegorm* was first discovered and documented by Commander Jacques Cousteau 15 years after she sank, during his 1956 expedition in which he explored the Red Sea in his vessel the *Calypso,* frequently diving for wrecks and recording them. Since then, thousands of divers have explored the *Thistlegorm,* making this cargo ship one of the most coveted, well-known diving sites in the world.

The wreck's location is easily accessible from Sharm el Sheikh.

Though the metal hull is completely covered by corals, and thousands of fish of every kind make this artificial reef their home, the ship's cargo is still perfectly visible, and no diver should miss the fascinating experience of visiting the wreck. The size and interest of the ship are such that you will need to make at least two dives in order to explore most of the ship and get an idea of her cargo.

For safety purposes, it is essential to tie a lead cord to the superstructures to help you descend and surface again. Currents can change direction and strength in just a few minutes, and a diver could be pulled far from his boat. The first dive includes an exploration of the

125 top Albert Falco and his diving companion Dumas were the first to see the submerged hull of the Thistlegorm. *They had embarked on the* Calypso *with Jacques Cousteau for the 1956 expedition that explored the Red Sea.*

125 bottom left The windlasses for weighing anchor are still perfectly visible on the foredeck. The metallic structure of the chains, which have little encrustation, can still be seen.

125 bottom right Two paravanes are secured to the sides of the mainmast. These devices, similar to small torpedoes, were used to render harmless any surface percussion mines.

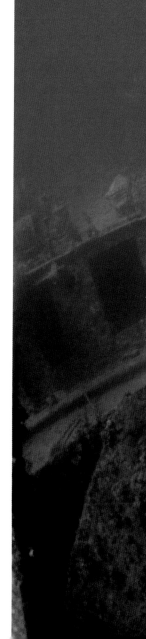

outer part of the wreck. Starting from the bow, you'll immediately see the large capstan and its chains on the deck. It was used to hoist the two heavy anchors, one of which, on the left, is still in place dangling from the bulwark, while the other is on the seabed about 230 ft (70 m) from the bow.

Proceeding towards the stern, on the upper deck you'll find two tank cars, near which are compact groups of batfish. You then come to the mainmast, which is split and lies on the decks, with a mine-sweeping paravane torpedo on either side.

Along the port side, which is usually more exposed to the current, you'll see a large, whirling group of big barracudas that create a silvery vortex.

Near the surface in this area are schools of carangids and seabream, snouts against the current as they lie in ambush for passing fusiliers. Two more train cars are on the sides of the entry to the second hold; they are encrusted with soft and hard corals.

The bridge is almost completely impassable, but its outer corridors create an evocative passageway, where you'll see numerous butter-flyfish.

After passing over a contorted metal canopy, where you'll usually see a few spotted flatheads, you'll come to the place where the bombs exploded, splitting the hull in two: the after section is slightly tilted to the port side and is about 49 ft (15

m) from the rest of the wreck. This is one of the most interesting, photo-genic parts of the *Thistlegorm*. On the sea floor, emerging from the wreckage, you'll see two light tanks, and swimming above them, a dense group of butterflyfish with long dor-sal fins and yellow, white and black bands. Some 66 ft (20 m) from the port side bulwark, resting on the sea floor, is one of the two locomotives that were loaded onto the deck; it is surrounded by a group of parrotfish using their sturdy beaks to pull off the hard corals. The inside of the boiler has become a shelter for thou-sands of glassfish.

The after section is perhaps the

most colorful of the entire wreck. Enormous alcyonarians hang from the framework, and amongst them clouds of silvery glassfish dart jerki-ly, creating gleams of light, angelfish swim slowly, curiously approaching divers, and all around there is a constant flashing of fish of every form and color. Large anemones, colonized by numerous clownfish, grow on the bulwarks and grip the contorted wreckage.

On the upper deck, the carriages of heavy weapons have given hard and soft corals a substratum where they can grow vigorously. This is the realm of groupers. Various large Malabar groupers will approach,

126 top right The explosion caused one of the two locomotives located above no. 4 hold to be thrown overboard. Today, you can see it on the sandy floor about 66 ft (20 m) from the port side of the ship.

126 bottom The holds contained large-caliber projectiles, including airplane bombs, grenades, anti-tank mines and mortars.

126-127 Two tank cars are still in their original position next to the hatch of no. 1 hold. They almost certainly contained fuel supplies for the many automobiles on board.

127 top In the foreground is the stairway that led to the forecastle. The metallic structures exposed to the current offer an ideal substratum for the vigorous growth of soft corals. The smokestack is completely covered with bright red sponges.

and when the current is weak, you may have an exceptional encounter with giant groupers almost 6.5 ft (2 m) long, weighing 550-660 lbs (250-300 kg).

The second dive of the day includes a visit to the holds, where you will need a good underwater flashlight. Starting from the bow again, go into no. 1 hold, where the lower level contains large tires, field generators, parts of airplane fuselages, rubber boots and cases of rifles. On the upper level are some Morris automobiles that are still in good condition, as well as BSA motorcycles. These are examples of a special model built for long trips on rough North African tracks.

This may be the most plundered part of the wreck — disrespectful divers have carried off many pieces of motor vehicles, perhaps as senseless souvenirs.

In the lowest levels of no. 2 hold, you'll find other motorcycles loaded onto trucks, with a large number of upright motorcycles in the upper portion. The atmosphere in this area is extremely fascinating, as the vehicles are in amazingly good condition.

In the narrow passageway that connects the two holds, numerous roofless Jeeps are lined up, almost all of them with their windshields perfectly intact. In the two cargo

128 top The lower level of no. 2 hold contains numerous Bedford trucks.

128 center A scuba diver illuminates the driver's seat of a heavy vehicle.

128 bottom The photograph shows the back of a Bedford truck. The motorcycles have been stripped of all accessories.

levels of no. 3 hold, you'll find piles of projectiles and bombs of various sizes and calibers, along with cases of other matériel. Apart from a few groupers, schools of 0fish, and some swarms of glassfish, not many fish frequent the holds.

A plea to anyone who dives on the wreck of the *Thistlegorm:* Resist any temptation to take a "piece of history" home with you. It would be profaning this testimony of the tragic past, a testimony that belongs to all.

128-129 The level of no. 1 hold closest to the surface contains rows of Morris automobiles, which were used by the British Eighth Army.

129 top BSA motorcycles, almost of which are the WDM20 model, were built for use under extreme environmental conditions.

GHIANNIS D

BY VINCENZO PAOLILLO

TECHNICAL CARD

TYPE OF WRECK	Cargo ship
NATIONALITY	Greek
YEAR OF CONSTRUCTION	1969
DATE SUNK	April 19, 1983
CAUSE OF SINKING	Struck a reef
LOCATION	Reef Abu Nuhas, Egypt
DISTANCE FROM SHORE	Close to the reef
MINIMUM DEPTH	33 ft / 10 m
MAXIMUM DEPTH	88 ft / 27 m
LENGTH	324 ft / 100 m

The *Ghiannis D* lies in the northwest corner of the Abu Nuhas Reef. She was a 2932-ton cargo ship, 325 ft (100 m) long, 52 ft (16 m) wide. Her diesel engine drove twin propellers that gave her a cruising speed of over 12 knots an hour and provided easy maneuverability.

She was built in Japan in 1969 and was initially called the *Shoyo Maru* (traces of this name appear on the bow), then the *Mar Kos*, after being sold to a Greek company.

When the *Mar Kos* changed hands in the early 1980s, her new owners named her the *Ghiannis,* the name she bore when she sank.

The large "D" on the smokestack has caused confusion. Some believe the ship was called the *Dana,* while others think the D referred to the Danae shipping company. The D did refer to a shipping company: the Dumarc Shipping and Trading Corporation of Piraeus.

The shipwreck occurred on April 19, 1983, during the *Ghiannis'* voyage from Rijeka in the Adriatic to Hodeida on the Yemeni coast of the Red Sea. She was carrying a cargo that some believe was softwood and others cables and large pipes; probably it was both.

How, in recent years, a well-equipped ship sailing in broad daylight could slam at full speed into a reef shown on every nautical map is a mystery. The only thing we know is that after passing the Straits of Gubal the captain went below to take a nap. Then suddenly the ship was seen veering off course and heading straight for the reefs of Abu Nuhas. The impact was extremely violent. The *Ghiannis* rose up onto the reef and thus did not sink immediately, which made it possible to rescue the entire crew. She then remained stuck on the reef for 6 weeks before being dragged to the bottom by currents and rough waves.

The wreck of the *Ghiannis* is essentially broken into three sections. The bow lies on its port side 59 ft (18

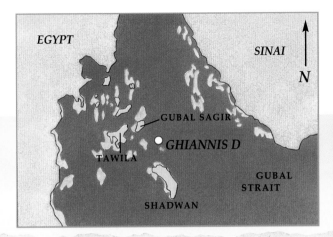

33 ft / 10 m

88 ft / 27 m

130 bottom
The bow is resting on the port side. The anchor chain that the sailors tossed into the sea to secure the ship to the reef is still hanging from the hawsehole.

131 center
The letter "D," which stands for the Dumarc Company, is still visible on the smokestack.

GHIANNIS D

m) deep, while a forward section right behind the bow has been reduced to a mass of wreckage. The after section with the quarterdeck, lying at a maximum depth of about 88 ft (27 m), is perfectly intact, with the smokestack bent to the left at a 45° angle.

The whole wreck is colonized by beautiful red, violet, blue, white and orange alcyonarians that have covered all the structures, galleries, capstans, windows and ropes, and clouds of swallowtail seaperch swim all around.

Start your dive from the stern. Swim a little way out toward the open sea in order to be able to fully appreciate the magnificent, still-intact structure, adorned with festoons of corals, sponges, and alcyonarians, the beautiful smokestack, the trestle of the starboard cargo boom, and a large upside-down "U" mast that almost touches the surface.

Then ascend up along the hull to enter the quarterdeck with its large bridge, or descend through the hatches at the base of the smokestack into the engine room.

Getting in is not difficult. It's not totally dark, as a bit of light filters in from the smokestack, but you'll still

132 In this evocative view of the stern, the great starboard boom can be seen in the clear water.

133 top The amidships area is the most deteriorated as a result of violent breakers.

133 center In this photo, taken a few years ago, colonization had just begun.

133 bottom left All the wreck's structures are covered with hard and soft corals.

133 bottom right One of the numerous magnificent alcyonarians that have colonized the structure stands out in this photo.

need a good flashlight. The place is impressive, with its engines, gangways, lathes and work surfaces, all perfectly conserved, in the midst of which swim schools of glassfish that dart quickly away as you arrive. But be very careful, as the 45° incline creates enormous equilibrium problems for divers.

Coming out, continue to explore the quarterdeck, also adorned with sponges, alcyonarians, and sea anemones with clownfish. Coral fish move busily all around, including batfish, lionfish, parrotfish, butterflyfish, angelfish, groupers, mullets, and especially clouds of glassfish and swallowtail seaperch.

Before you reach the amidships section, look at the beautiful view created by the port-side boom. Cracked and lying on the sand, it is covered by an explosion of alcyonarians.

You will then cross the destroyed area. In the midst of the wreckage, also colonized by alcyonarians, you're likely to see large groupers, angelfish, morays, and especially lionfish (Pterois). You will then come to the truly impressive bow with its capstans and the mast pointing out to sea.

Particularly lovely is the sight of the keel and the massive anchor chain, which the crew must have released into the water after the collision in an attempt to secure the ship to the reef.

134 top The holds are populated by clouds of glassfish.

134 bottom left The ladder that runs up the side of the ship has become home to various colorful life forms.

134 bottom right The wreck is inhabited by various forms of animal life, which find an ideal habitat within the hull. This photo shows a surgeonfish placidly swimming across the spectral background of the ship's interior.

134-135 The port side boom cracked and fell overboard when the ship sank, and now lies in the sand.

135 top A scuba diver who ventures inside the wreck will find it somewhat difficult to keep his balance owing to the ship's tilt.

CARNATIC

BY CLAUDIO CANGINI

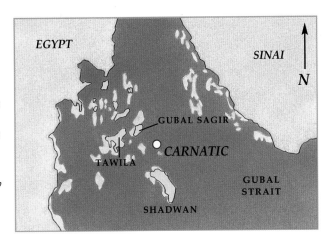

66 ft / 20 m

85 ft / 26 m

The *Carnatic* was launched in December 1862. The Peninsular & Oriental Steam Navigation Company, a London shipping company, commissioned her construction at Samuda Brothers shipyard, and she was entered in the naval register in early 1863 and insured with Lloyd's. In April 1862, the *Carnatic* hoisted anchor for her maiden voyage, which took her from Southampton into the Atlantic Ocean, then to the Mediterranean and Alexandria, Egypt. She was then used to carry passengers and goods to and from India.

The *Carnatic* was a steam sailing ship, a hybrid type of construction many naval designers adopted in the 19th century. It bowed to the advent of engines without forgoing the reliability and greater speed guaranteed by the wind. During her first mission,

137 bottom The Carnatic *foundered on the Abu Nuhas reef for two nights. The captain underestimated the damage to the hull and did not evacuate the ship immediately, a decision that cost 27 passengers their lives.*

wind and coal took the steamer from England to Colombo, Sri Lanka in less than two months, a record time for that era. Her coal-fired boiler and the power behind the Humphrys & Tennant engine generated almost 2500 hp and gave the propeller shaft enough power to ensure a speed of over 12 knots an hour. The two masts, over 40 ft (12 m) high, supported impressively

large sails that allowed the *Carnatic* to travel much faster than through mechanical propulsion. The British Merchant Marine used hybrid boats on the India route; in any weather, for example when winds were calm, they could still maintain the required speed, and they guaranteed punctuality for cargoes of perishable goods or mail.

TECHNICAL CARD	
TYPE OF WRECK	*Passenger and cargo steamship*
NATIONALITY	*English*
YEAR OF CONSTRUCTION	*1862*
DATE SUNK	*September 14, 1869*
CAUSE OF SINKING	*Struck a reef*
LOCATION	*Sha'ab Abu Reef, Egypt*
DISTANCE FROM SHORE	*Close to the reef*
MINIMUM DEPTH	*66 ft / 20 m*
MAXIMUM DEPTH	*85 ft / 26 m*
LENGTH	*About 295 ft / 90 m*

*138 top left
The corals that
cover the wreck can
be seen on the
metal structures of
the hull. The large
leaks that caused
the ship to sink
make it easy to
enter the holds.*

*138 top right
Regardless of what
caused the
shipwreck, exploring
a sunken ship
creates a sense of
respect for what the
boat represented
when she still plied
the waves.*

*138 bottom
The Carnatic's
streamlined bow is
very evident here.
The large hole in the
center marks the
bowsprit seating.*

*139 This photo
shows the steamer's
stern: we can clearly
see the rudder fin
and the blades of the
great propeller that
drove the ship at a
maximum speed of
12 knots.*

The *Carnatic* was a little less than 295 ft (90 m) long and about 33 ft (10 m) wide. Her keel drew 17 ft (5.3 m) upright, and her total tonnage was 1800 tons. The ship's designer made her low and streamlined; the transom was wide and not very tapered, a characteristic of the fastest sailing vessels; her centrally located smokestack gave her an unusual appearance; and her bow was adorned with a wooden figurehead.

The voyage that spelled the *Carnatic*'s end was to take her from the coast of Egypt to India: she hoisted anchor on September 12, 1869 from Suez, headed for Bombay and then Calcutta. She carried a cargo of bales of cotton, copper ingots of various sizes, about 44-66 lbs (20-30 kg) each, bags of letters, and about 40,000 sovereigns in her safe, worth millions of euros in today's values. The hold also contained oval bottles of London soda water, with their final destination incised on the opaline glass: Calcutta or Bombay. She was also loaded with numerous bottles of wine that bore a raised number 2, perhaps the lot code.

The exact number of persons on board is uncertain, but it does appear that there were about 40 passengers (some sources report that there was a total of 230 people on board, including crew and passengers). In the pre-dawn hours of September 13, a vedette sighted a line of reefs along the *Carnatic*'s route, a clear sign of a shallow seabed. Captain Jones gave the order back up and bear hard to port, thus avoiding the main reef at Abu Nuhas, but the ship's great momentum led her to strike and run aground on a hard coral pinnacle below the surface, where she remained trapped. Captain Jones did not feel the situation was serious and unloaded only a portion of the ship's cargo on launches in order to lighten the vessel. Another ship from the P & O Company was expected to pass through shortly, and it was decided to wait for her before transferring the passengers.

In the meantime, water began to leak into the *Carnatic*'s bilges. Meals were served regularly, and passengers prepared to spend another night on board. Before dawn on September 14, water entered the engine room, damaging the boiler. The tragic fate of the vessel was now clear, and passengers began to be evacuated. By late morning, the strong wind and powerful waves caused the ship to sink stern first. All she left on the surface was a part of the bow. Twenty-seven people died in the shipwreck. The rest of the *Carnatic*'s human cargo reached Shadwan Island and was rescued by the *Sumatra* the next day. The ship remained in almost vertical position for a few months, then a storm completed the work.

Today the *Carnatic* lies on the sea floor on her port side at a depth of 85 ft (26 m). She lies at the base of Sha'ab Abu Nuhas reef, a mass of hard corals rising up 2 miles (3.2 km) north of Shadwan Island. Abu Nuhas is sadly famous for sinking numerous ships, and today divers from all over the world head there to visit this ship cemetery. Coral has

CARNATIC

140 *The sea has eroded the wooden tables in the main deck passageway. Today the metal cross-beams are home to corals.*

141 *top A good underwater torch is indispensable for exploring areas where the sun does not penetrate, in this case the hold and a portion of the cargo.*

141 *center Some of the less explored parts of the ship still contain a few bottles of soda water or wine that were part of the* Carnatic's *cargo. Shipwrecks are pages of history swallowed by the sea, and divers who have the good fortune to be able to leaf through these pages have the duty to preserve their integrity.*

141 *bottom Clouds of glassfish (Parapriacanthus guentheri) live inside the hull of the* Carnatic. *These little fish take shelter in the darkest crevices of the structures during the day, and when dusk falls they come out in search of the zooplankton on which they feed. They are one of the highest expressions of group survival strategy.*

completely colonized the *Carnatic's* structures, but her shape is still perfectly reconizable. It's not especially difficult to enter the ship, and especially near the bow, you can see spectacular swarms of glassfish moving in unison as the groupers pursue them.

Now the wood has crumbled and the beams that were the deck's framework look like the bars of an enormous cage, with rays of sunlight creating spectacular patterns within. Clusters of alcyonarians are everywhere. The propeller blades are especially lovely, embellished by tufts of red and yellow soft corals. Even hard corals flourish and are growing luxuriantly, in particular on the stern and the bulwarks most exposed to the light. Every day at dusk, millions of glassfish create an extraordinarily impressive sight as they come out of the holds and venture into the open water to eat. Lying in wait for them are dozens of lionfish hovering about, moving their feather-like fins.

Almost nothing remains of the cargo. If you dive onto this spectacular wreck, the only things you should bring back are the images and thrills that this page from history offers you.

CHRISOULA K.

BY MASSIMO BICCIATO

TECHNICAL CARD	
TYPE OF WRECK	Cargo ship
NATIONALITY	Greek
YEAR OF CONSTRUCTION	1954
DATE SUNK	August 31, 1981
CAUSE OF SINKING	Struck a reef
LOCATION	Sha'ab Abu Nuhas Reef, Egypt
DISTANCE FROM SHORE	Close to the reef
MINIMUM DEPTH	62 ft / 19 m
MAXIMUM DEPTH	88 ft / 27 m
LENGTH	321 ft / 98 m

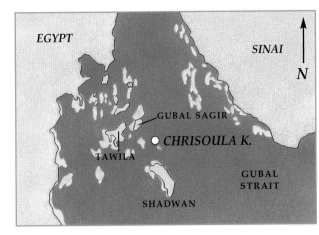

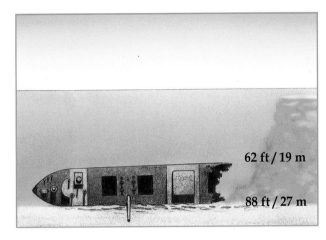

62 ft / 19 m

88 ft / 27 m

The *Chrisoula K.* was a cargo ship built in Germany at the Baltic port of Lübeck. She was 321 ft (98 m) long and 46 ft (15 m) wide, displaced 3,720 tons and was powered by a 9-cylinder 2,700-hp diesel engine built by Masch, Augusta-Nuremberg, a firm located in Augusta in the heart of Bavaria. She was launched in 1954 under the name *Dora Oldendorf.* In 1970, a different shipping company acquired her and renamed her *Anna B.* She sailed under this name until 1979. Then Clarion Company Marina, a Greek shipping company, acquired the *Anna B.* This company renamed her the *Chrisoula K.*

In August 1981, Captain Kanellis was in Italy on board ship to complete loading a cargo of Italian tiles headed for Jeddah, Saudi Arabia. When loading was complete, the *Chrisoula K.* headed out to sea on what would be her last voyage. She was 200 miles (330 km) away from the Suez Canal. Once she reached the strait and completed all transit formalities, she began sailing toward the Straits of Gubal.

After arriving in the Red Sea, after two days of uninterrupted command duty, Captain Kanellis decided to give himself a well-deserved rest and turned the ship over to his second in command.

With the port of Jeddah 600 miles (960 km) away, the *Chrisoula K.* sailed at full speed southward, when on 31 August 1981, a deafening crash signaled the ship's demise.

Owing to a navigational error of a few degrees, the *Chrisoula K.* had plowed into the northeast side of the reef at Sha'ab Abu Nuhas, a coral plateau difficult to see in a calm sea.

The ship was irreparably damaged by the tremendous impact, so violent that it completely ripped off the bow, which remained for years atop the reef, until gales completely destroyed it.

As you dive into the water, the first thing you'll see is the wreck with her stern leaning well over to starboard, while the rest of the ship is resting upright in sailing position.

Begin your detailed exploration in the deeper area, where the unique stern is located at a depth of 88 ft (27 m). Here you'll see the rudder and the enormous four-bladed propeller. If you follow the starboard side (right side from the stern), come up to a shallower depth, you'll find the mainmast resting on the sea

144 top left Entering the engine room requires much caution and an excellent flashlight.

144 bottom left The entire after section is resting on its starboard side, while the rest of the ship is upright.

144 top right A large capstan that was used to lower cables is visible toward the stern, along with a vertical windlass and sturdy bollards.

144 bottom right The Greek ship's mainmast is lying perpendicular to the wreck. Magnificent alcyonarians cover the crosstrees.

floor, with the smokestack, at a depth of a little over 63 ft (19 m). From here you can reach the openings in the hold, where the cargo of tiles was located, now heaped chaotically within the hull.

Being careful not to raise the thin layer of dust, go into the engine room, where the large 9-cylinder engine stands imperiously; even though it is covered with rust, it still exudes an aura of mechanical power.

All around are various pieces of equipment. The interior of the ship is especially spectacular owing to

the dense schools of glassfish *(Parapriacanthus guentheri)* darting rapidly in the shadows.

To get in, you'll need a flashlight, as the little light that filters in from the portholes and loading hatches is not enough to illuminate the interior.

Proceeding along what remains of the upper deck, you'll come to the bow area, which has been completely devastated by the tides. Here a mass of widely scattered wreckage is all that remains of the beautiful, slender bow that once plied the waves of this sea.

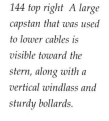

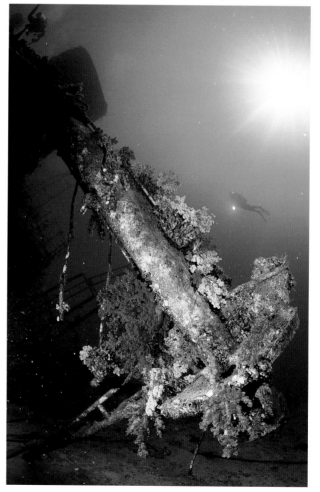

144-145 The ship's bow is reduced to a heap of scattered metal. After the accident, the bow remained grounded on the top of the reef until 1986, when the furious breakers that battered it incessantly finally sank it.

145 top Right after the accident, the port side anchor was dropped in hopes of keeping the ship moored to the reef, while the starboard anchor remained in the hawsehole, as can be seen in this photograph.

CHRISOULA K.

NUMIDIA

BY KURT AMSLER

One of the best places for diving in the Red Sea, but also one of the least accessible, is certainly the El Akhawein Islands (Brothers Islands). The wrecks of two ships lie among dense schools of fish in this surreal, pristine coral landscape: the *Numidia,* a fascinating wreck from 1901, and the *Aïda,* which sank in 1911.

The two little Brothers Islands, which are are in the open sea, surrounded by a narrow coastal reef, emerge from an abyss more than 3280 ft (1000 m) deep. Since 1883 there has been a lighthouse on Big Brother (yes! the larger island), which acted as a guide for ships of that period. Despite this, many ships have met a sad end here.

Most have been lost forever,

TECHNICAL CARD	
TYPE OF WRECK	Cargo ship
NATIONALITY	British
YEAR OF CONSTRUCTION	1901
DATE SUNK	July 21, 1901
CAUSE OF SINKING	Struck a reef
LOCATION	North of Brothers Islands, Egypt
DISTANCE FROM SHORE	Close to the reef
MINIMUM DEPTH	39 ft / 12 m
MAXIMUM DEPTH	230 ft / 70 m
LENGTH	492 ft / 150 m

swallowed by the abyss that lies beyond the steep drop-off that abuts the reef platform. However, two ships that foundered on the precipice are accessible to scuba divers when conditions are right. As the Brothers Islands are almost constantly swept by waves and currents, making it impossible to dive during the winter

months, the two wrecks are still practically unexplored, especially the *Numidia,* as she lies right on the northern tip, where the breakers crash and the current is strongest.

The beautifully named steamship *Numidia* was 492 ft (150 m) long and 59 ft (18 m) wide. When she left Liverpool, Great Britain, in July 1901,

146 top The wreck of the Numidia *lies right at the northern tip of the larger island (Big Brother). A lighthouse built here in 1883 is an indispensable guide for navigators.*

no one, least of all Captain J. Craig, could imagine that this would be her last voyage. She had not plied many waters; in fact this was only her second voyage after being launched at D&W Henderson Shipyard in Glasgow. In addition to other goods, the *Numidia* carried railroad tracks and railroad car wheels and axles. The ship was headed for Calcutta, on the classic Irish Sea-Atlantic-Mediterranean route that then traversed the Suez Canal and Red Sea to enter the Indian Ocean.

But destiny awaited. On 21 July, the *Numidia* struck the north point of the larger of the Brother Islands. History is silent on what caused the accident. Considering that the weather had been good for weeks and the sea was calm, the suspected culprit is a navigational error.

Whatever the cause was, the ship, which had a gross tonnage of 6390 tons, ran aground so firmly on the coral reef that she remained there for more than 16 days. As we can see from Lloyd's documents, all items of value were successfully salvaged during this period. Afterwards, the *Numidia* collapsed for good, sinking stern-first into the depths.

The wreck can be seen at the level of the reef, with fragments of the bow and a train wheel. Starting at a depth of 46 ft (15 m), the body of the ship gradually begins to take shape.

Train wheels are lying everywhere amongst the hard coral formations, and you can even admire two of them covered with marvelous soft corals. The *Numidia* lies on a slope of the coral reef, and including her propeller, she reaches a depth of 230 ft (70 m). The entire fore section of the ship has transformed into an enchanted coral garden, and the lower pas-

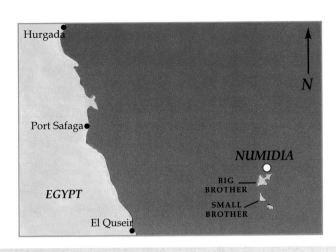

39 ft / 12 m

230 ft / 70 m

146 bottom The fore section of the ship viewed from the superstructures. The wooden coverings and tables on the deck have been completely corroded by long exposure to the sea.

148 *Currents are often powerful here on the northern tip of Big Brother, encouraging the proliferation of hard and soft corals throughout the wreck.*

149 top left *The cargo was mostly railroad materials. Two enormous train wheels and several sections of rail lie on the sloping reef.*

sageways, the bulwark rail, and lifeboat davits are thickly covered with soft corals.

You can visit the superstructures, one level after another, with no particular problems.

In the central part of the hull are the completely empty holds and the mainmast. The derricks lie both lengthwise and across the deck and over the now gaping hatches. Beginning at the mainmast, the wreck sinks down another 66 ft (20 m), where the stern and propeller lie, well beyond the range of amateur divers!

Given her marvelous corals, the *Numidia* can rightfully claim to be one of the most beautiful wrecks in the Red Sea.

149 center left *The holds of the Numidia, whose cargo was loaded using large capstans and derricks, are now completely empty.*

149 top right *A diver explores the starboard side. Nature has taken over the ship since she came to rest on the sea floor.*

149 bottom left *The lifeboat davits are clearly distinguishable in the gangway and along the railing at the Numidia's waist.*

149 bottom right *This is the railing along the starboard side. Here as everywhere, metal structures are covered in corals.*

TUGBOAT

BY MASSIMO BICCIATO

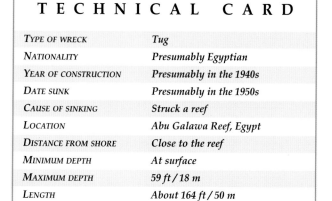

TECHNICAL CARD	
TYPE OF WRECK	Tug
NATIONALITY	Presumably Egyptian
YEAR OF CONSTRUCTION	Presumably in the 1940s
DATE SUNK	Presumably in the 1950s
CAUSE OF SINKING	Struck a reef
LOCATION	Abu Galawa Reef, Egypt
DISTANCE FROM SHORE	Close to the reef
MINIMUM DEPTH	At surface
MAXIMUM DEPTH	59 ft / 18 m
LENGTH	About 164 ft / 50 m

The Abu Galawa coral reef is located to the east between the little harbor at Ras Qulan and the promontory of Ras Banas. In August 1990, the wreck of a small tugboat was found by chance in the northern part of this reef. We know nothing of the Abu Galawa tugboat, which for unknown reasons smashed into the wall of the reef, causing the boat irreparable damage, with a great leak in the forward area.

How the boat got into this intricate coral maze is truly a mystery. Perhaps she was trying to rescue a damaged ship, but we can only imagine the circumstances. One thing for certain is that the tugboat collided violently with the corals. We can assume that the accident happened sometime in the 1950s, as various objects found inside the boat date back to that period.

The wreck is easy to identify even from the outside, as part of the bow breaks the surface and is resting on the reef, while the rest of the hull follows the slope down 59 ft (18 m), where the stern and the propeller are half-buried. You can reach your diving point either on a raft or by jumping directly into the water from the boat's mooring place, conveniently close by.

This especially easy dive should pose no problems even for beginners, as the interior is now empty and of no interest except for the presence of a dense school of glassfish. The best place to view the wreck in its entirety is the after area, where you can hover in the open water. As visibility is almost always excellent from here, you can get a full view of the hull, leaning against the wall.

You will note that the wreck, which is still in good condition, leans slightly toward her starboard side, and looks like one of those old post-war tugboats with their tapered profiles. Various items present when the wreck was discovered have been thoughtlessly stolen, including a beautiful 1920s fan and various porthole windows. If you're interested, you can enter the engine room, being very careful not to raise

150 bottom left Magnificent hard coral formations have colonized the tugboat's bow area.

150 top right From the stern, you'll see that the wreck tilts slightly to starboard. The afternoon light fully illuminates the ship's silhouette.

150 bottom right The stern section of the hull lies on the white sand floor, 59 ft (18 m) below the surface.

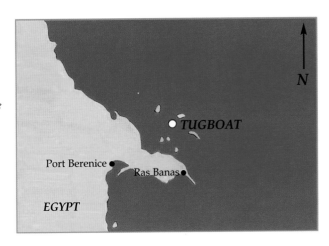

the heavy layer of sediment everywhere.

But the most interesting part is certainly the outside, which is totally encrusted with rich hard coral formations and sponges and surrounded by a profusion of coral fish.

Some truck tires attached to the stern as bumpers are now a den for groups of lionfish (*Pterois miles*), and the smokestack has become the permanent dwelling of a small red grouper. Below the stern near the propeller, you'll often see a large grouper hidden among the wreckage.

The absolutely best time to dive onto the Abu Galawa tugboat is at sunset, when the little wreck springs to life with the swarms of fish that emerge at dusk.

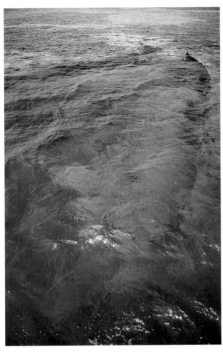

152-153 The ship looks like an old, tapered tugboat from right after the war. Here you can appreciate the excellent condition of the hull.

153 top left When the sea is calm and the water clear, you can clearly see the tugboat's silhouette from the surface.

153 top right This large truck tire, secured to the stern area and probably used as a bumper, is now covered with a thin red sponge.

153 bottom The narrow smokestack rising from the amidships area is home to a grouper tha lives inside it. Hard coral continues to grow on the rest of the wreckage.

CARGO SHIP

BY MASSIMO BICCIATO

This is a Russian cargo ship that sank in the mid-1970s in the lagoon southeast of Zabargad Island. For years, the only traces of the wreck were the three lifeboats abandoned on the beach in the inlets northeast and southwest of the island. They were not wreckage tossed by the sea, but English-type aluminum boats about 23 ft (7 m) long, equipped with manual bilge pumps.

On a windy day in September, with waves forming within the lagoon, an iron section occasionally surfaced from the foam, something indefinite and yet distinct from the reef environment, a small piece of metal that appeared and disappeared with the flow of the waves. Just a few minutes later came the discovery, when the form of a small cargo ship emerged, resting on the sea floor in perfectly upright position with its prow facing the open sea.

Your first sensation as you observe the wreck is that it must have been seeking shelter in the little lagoon, and this must have been due to a breakdown. This theory was later confirmed by a number of decisive details: the stern seemed devastated by an enormous hole with contorted wreckage blown outwards, the davits for lowering the lifeboats were dismantled and also turned outwards, and finally the chains of the anchors had been dropped from their hawse-holes in a last ditch attempt to secure the ship in the only place of shelter. These details support the theory of an onboard accident that caused a fatal breakdown, with the ship

finally sinking. These preliminary snapshots are the only evidence of the desperate attempts of the captain and crew to save the ship, which finally surrendered to the devastating power of a gale and a reef that offered no escape, with the waves finally closing over them forever.

This dive can be made using a rubber raft moored near the wreck. You should dive in the early afternoon when the light is optimal. About 230 ft (70 m) of the ship is resting on a sandy sea floor at a maximum depth of 82 ft (25 m). About three quarters of the ship is intact, with the bow section partially separated from the rest of the hull and leaning on its port side due to the strong undertow. You should go

154 top On the upper deck, viewed from the bow, you can see the openings to the holds, where cases of electrical materials were found. In the background are the supports to which the lifeboats were attached.

154 bottom A group of divers explores the after area of the Russian cargo ship. There is an enormous gash on the starboard side of the ship, most probably caused by an explosion in the engine room.

82 ft / 25 m

TECHNICAL CARD

TYPE OF WRECK	Cargo ship
NATIONALITY	Presumably Russian
YEAR OF CONSTRUCTION	Unknown
DATE SUNK	In the mid-1950s
CAUSE OF SINKING	Explosion and struck a reef
LOCATION	Zabargad Island, Egypt
DISTANCE FROM SHORE	16 ft / 5 m
MINIMUM DEPTH	At surface
MAXIMUM DEPTH	82 ft / 25 m
LENGTH	About 230 ft / 70 m

156 left The after transom is completely covered with coral formations that are rapidly taking over the surface of the wreck.

156-157 The bow transom still has sturdy bollards secured to the structure and a windlass for the after anchor, its chain still taut.

directly to the stern area, where you can observe the two four-bladed propellers half submerged in the sand, and from here, proceeding along the starboard side, the enormous hole caused by the presumed explosion. When you reach the bow, go back up to the main deck, where four half-open hatches lead to the holds, which once contained cases of electrical materials. Continuing, you'll come to the bridge, where you'll find what remains of the telephone, radio station and the place where the chart table was located. Going on to explore the stern, you'll pass the main deck, where two cargo booms and various windlasses are located, encrusted with hard corals and alcyonarians. Once you reach the aft, on the starboard side you'll find the hatch leading to the engine room, which you can enter with a flashlight. Move with extreme care, as it is easy to raise the dense, rusty dust that covers all the bulkheads. When the dive is over, go to the mainmast located in the center of the ship, and from here ascend back to the surface. Take a last look at the entire wreck as it lies on the sea floor.

157 top left This spare rudder is in the ship's engine room. It was easily accessible so it could be promptly replaced in case the main rudder failed.

157 top right The ship's lantern was originally in the bridge. Unfortunately, it was pulled out and thrown onto the sea floor by divers with no sensitivity or respect.

157 bottom left One of the ship's bathrooms is located on the upper deck. This photo clearly shows the layer of rust that covers all the iron sections of the wreck.

157 bottom right This photo shows one of the two compasses oil-bath that were on the outer deck of the ship when she was discovered.

BLUE BELT

BY MASSIMO BICCIATO

The *Blue Belt* is a gigantic freighter launched in 1950, built in the Howaldts-Werke A. G. shipyard in Hamburg. Known as the "Toyota Wreck," she is 341 ft (103.82 m) long and 46 ft (14 m) wide, with a tonnage of 2,399 tons. On December 1, 1977 she was sailing from the port of Jeddah headed toward Port Sudan, carrying 181 automobiles, 6 trucks, various trailers, and spare parts for Toyota automobiles.

The dynamics of the accident are still unclear, as large ships like this usually follow a route that runs through the central channel of the Red Sea, far from all danger. Yet this ship foundered on the reef of Sha'ab Su'adi, just a few miles from the coast, in a stretch of sea that was absolutely prohibited to navigation by large tonnage ships. The cause may be human error, probably as a result of poor conditions or visibility, but it may also have been a clandestine transport of automobiles that would have been unloaded in the little *marsa*, or port, of Arakiyai, not far from the coast. Just a little north of

158 top Observing the wreck from above, we can see the engines of the trucks that were part of the **Blue Belt's** *cargo, thrown overboard in an effort to lighten the ship's load during desperate attempts to save her.*

158 bottom left The gigantic port side anchor of the **Blue Belt** *is still in the hawsehole, while the starboard anchor was lowered in a frantic attempt to secure the ship to the reef. Small soft coral formations are developing in the keel.*

TYPE OF WRECK	Cargo ship
NATIONALITY	Saudi-Arabian
YEAR OF CONSTRUCTION	1950
DATE SUNK	December 5, 1977
CAUSE OF SINKING	Struck a reef
LOCATION	Sha'ab Su'adi Reef, Sudan
DISTANCE FROM SHORE	Close to the reef
MINIMUM DEPTH	39 ft / 12 m
MAXIMUM DEPTH	272 ft / 83 m
LENGTH	About 1115 ft / 104 m

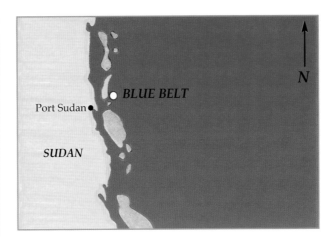

N

BLUE BELT

Port Sudan

SUDAN

39 ft / 12 m

272 ft / 83 m

the shipwreck, there is in fact a passage that leads directly into the *marsa*. What we know for certain is that for three long days the ship's crew tried in vain to save the *Blue Belt* and prevent her from sinking; they even threw vehicles overboard to lighten the load. All to no avail: on December 5, the *Blue Belt* capsized along the slope and came to rest perpendicular to the reef, her bow pointed west at a depth of 39 ft (12 m) and the stern facing east at a depth of 272 ft (83 m). The wreck is completely overturned, with the keel upward and the decks resting on the sea floor. On the top reef, you can see a truck trailer catapulted out by the impact. Use this for identification purposes. Starting from the bow, we can see the long anchor chain emerging from the port side hawsehole and disappearing on the reef, while the starboard anchor is still in place. The broad, flat keel shows the large rip that caused the *Blue Belt* to sink.

The stern is resting on the bottom, while the enormous rudder and large, 4-bladed propeller are facing upward at a depth of 243 ft (74 m). At a depth of 177 ft (54 m), the sea bed on which the wreck lies has created a broad ridge rising to 151 ft (46 m) from the surface. The forecastle is wedged in here, and two passages in this area connect to the opposite side. If you have a good flashlight, you can see some automobiles still attached to

160 top On the wreck's port side, you can see how the entire deck of the overturned ship lies on the coral reef. Encrusted ropes are still visible on the reef.

160 center This automobile is still for the most part intact. The driver's seat, steering wheel, and dashboard are still in place, and the passenger compartment is now home to a colony of anthias.

160 bottom Using a powerful flashlight, you can see several automobiles inside the hold near the stern, still secured to their rails. A pickup truck in perfect condition is also recognizable.

the rails, hanging from the top of the holds.

But the most surprising sight is the enormous pink alcyonarians that hang from above and a number of ropes floating in the water, also covered with violet alcyonarians. A dense school of carangids lives in this area. At the bow, you'll find various pick-ups and a truck whose iron sections have been colonized over the years by corals and alcyonarians . Glassfish have taken over the truck, surrounding it completely. On the opposite side of the ship, you'll see a small mast, the top and cross-tree lying on the bottom along with the remains of other automobiles.

160-161 Hard coral formations have colonized the automobile tires. In the foreground, you can see an extremely fragile branch of coral extending outward.

161 top Over time, fragile branches of hard coral are taking over all the iron surfaces. A millepore coral is slowly changing the form of a pickup's steering wheel.

UMBRIA

BY MASSIMO BICCIATO

TECHNICAL CARD

TYPE OF WRECK	Cargo and passenger ship
NATIONALITY	Italian
YEAR OF CONSTRUCTION	December 30, 1911
DATE SUNK	June 10, 1940
CAUSE OF SINKING	Scuttling
LOCATION	Close to Wingate Reef, Sudan
DISTANCE FROM SHORE	About 656 ft / 200 m from reef
MINIMUM DEPTH	At surface
MAXIMUM DEPTH	125 ft / 38 m
LENGTH	508 ft / 155 m

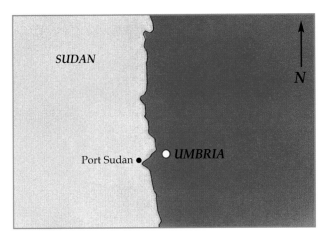

125 ft / 38 m

T he ship, whose original name was the *Bahía Blanca*, was launched by the Reiherst Schiffswerke shipyard on December 30, 1911 on behalf of Amerika Line, which sailed South American routes, especially to Argentina; she sailed these routes for a number of years. She was 508 ft (155 m) long and 59 ft (18 m) wide, with a gross tonnage of 10,128 tons. She was designed as a cargo and passenger ship, with 2400 berths in two classes with a central bridgehouse, two decks and two corridors. When World War I broke out, the *Bahía Blanca* was interned in the port of Buenos Aires, where she remained until 1918, when she was purchased by the Argentinean government, which used her until 1935. She was decommissioned and then purchased by the Italian government, which turned her over for operation by Società Italia of Genoa, which changed her name to the *Umbria*.

Thus began the new history of this ship, which was used to transport troops to the East African colonies. The *Umbria*'s last voyage began on May 28, 1940 from the ports of Genoa, Livorno, and Naples, where it loaded wartime materiel for the ports of Massawa and Assab, then headed to the Suez Canal with her holds loaded with 6,000 tons of bombs and 600 cases of detonators, incendiary bombs, 200 tons of high explosives, 100 tons of various weapons, plus 2000 tons of cement and three Fiat 1100 vehicles. On June 3 she reached Port Said for her last fuel reloading. Four days later, as

she was speeding south, she was stopped by two war units: the New Zealand cruiser *Leander* and the British sloop *Grimsby*, which forced her to land at Wingate reef, across from the harbor at Port Sudan; tension due to the impending war was increasing, and finally, on June 9 at 6:30 p.m. Eritrean time, Captain Lorenzo Muiesan (Trieste, class of 1895) went into his cabin and turned on the radio: an official communiqué confirmed the onset of hostilities around midnight that same day. Without hesitation, the captain called his orderly Danilo and ordered him to throw all the secret codes on board into the boiler. He then called engine master Costa and first officer

Zarli, and they together decided to immediately scuttle the ship without notifying the British. Shortly thereafter, Zarli asked the British official Stevens for official permission to conduct a normal rescue drill on board; the British soldiers guarding the cargo were alarmed by what was happening and immediately advised their superior that water was entering the holds. Stevens went to the captain's cabin to demand an explanation, and was told, "I'm sorry, Mr. Stevens, but I heard that war has broken out; the ship is sinking and the only thing you can do is collect your people and leave." A motorboat loaded with marines was immediately sent from the *Leander* and picked

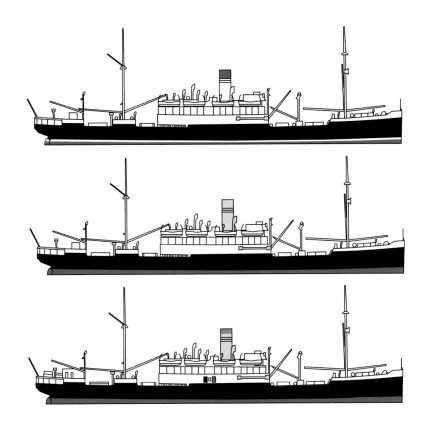

up Captain Muiesan and his crew. The *Umbria's* precious cargo sank in two hours, dispelling any fears that the ship might remain in enemy hands.

The *Umbria*, the stage for Italy's first heroic act during World War II, still lies there, resting on one side, with the lifeboat tackles emerging from the surface and the coral gradually taking over the wreckage. This is an especially beautiful dive, as the wreck is completely intact, with her starboard side just below the surface and the four davits emerging; nevertheless, you'll need a number of dives to explore her thoroughly. Starting from the stern, you can admire the great rudder and one of the two four-bladed propellers standing out against the deep blue sea. The second propeller, located about 98 ft (30 m) away, is half submerged in the muddy seabed. Continuing along to the left, you'll come to two holds containing the still neatly stacked bombs, immediately followed by the bridgehouse and the great smokestack that has broken off from it and rests on the sea floor. The deepest part of the dive, at a depth of about 115ft (35 m), follows

164-165 The aft quarter has been completely colonized by hard coral formations and colorful sponges that give the old wreckage an extremely vital appearance.

165 top left The Umbria's lovely bow rests majestically 59 ft (18 m) below the surface. From a distance, when the water is clear, you can see her distinctive sharp lines.

165 center left When the sea is calm and the water transparent, you can see the ship from the surface in all her majesty. The lifeboat davits break the water's surface.

165 bottom right The upper promenade deck located near the ship's bridgehouse can be seen even during a free dive.

165 center right This view of the wreck's aft area shows the great rudder and twin propellers.

165 bottom left The stern-rail area is completely covered by magnificent sponges and hard coral.

165

166 top The
ventilator is lying
on the sandy floor in
the amidships area
115 ft (35 m) deep.
Poor visibility does
not allow for long
visits to this area.

166 center left
Hard corals,
colorful sponges,
and a profusion of
marine life are
taking over the
wreck. Life around
the ship is frenetic,
and countless
species of coral fish
can be seen.

166 center right
The capstan for
handling cargo is
located near the
bow area. Small,
colorful formations
of soft corals are
slowly developing.

the muddy sea floor, where two of the eight lifeboats lie abandoned. Don't spend too much time here, as visibility is poor. Instead, continue to swim, keeping the side of the ship on your right, and you will soon come to the most interesting hold, which contained not only various construction materials, but also precious Fiat 1100 Lunghe vehicles.

You'll need a good flashlight in this hold. Move about very careful-ly, as the thick layer of rusty dust covering every structure is raised by any tiny movement of the water. In the next hold, you'll find mostly bottles of wine, bags of cement and airplane bombs. Then explore the fifth and last hold, which contains various airplane tires and spools of electric wire. You're near the beautiful bow, and if you look down lengthwise from the ship, you can see her magnificent tapered, aggres-sive line with the chain of the anchor dropped from the portside hawse-hole. From here, continue exploring along the deck to the first class promenade, from which you can enter the various rooms, including the restaurant, still imbued with the magical atmosphere of this wreck. The *Umbria*, a fragment of Italian history, continues to live and silently recount her fascinating adventure under the sea.

166 bottom The
protection for the
rudder power unit is
located below the aft
promenade.

166-167 This photo
shows a detail of the
aft area capstan,
utilized to maneuver
the cargo boom.

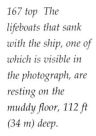

167 top The lifeboats that sank with the ship, one of which is visible in the photograph, are resting on the muddy floor, 112 ft (34 m) deep.

168 top This image shows two of the three 6 seater Fiat 1100 Lunghe, designed especially for the Italian colonies in Eritrea. The Turin automobile company produced this model from 1939 to 1948.

168 bottom left
The now empty mess deck is covered by a layer of rust, becoming a magical place where the rays of light that penetrate the portholes create sensational, evocative effects.

168 bottom right
In the galley, we can still see majolica-covered ovens. Access, which is quite difficult, is above no. 3 hold, where the automobiles are located.

169 top left This rear view of one of the vehicles shows the spare tire designed for the colonies, with cross-hatched tires required for desert driving.

169 bottom left
There were 360,000 bombs crammed into no. 4 hold. According to an estimate made after the sinking, if they had exploded, the entire east side of Port Sudan would have been submerged.

169 top right
The spacious holds contained goods of all kinds from Italy. This hold contained bottles of red wine, most of which are still intact, destined for the colonies.

169 bottom right
The ship's workshop contains two lathes, a large grindstone, a drill press, a counter with drawers and two vises, all still intact and covered with a thin layer of ferrous ooze.

NAZARIO SAURO

BY EGIDIO TRAINITO

TECHNICAL CARD	
TYPE OF WRECK	Cargo and passenger ship
NATIONALITY	Italian
YEAR OF CONSTRUCTION	1921
DATE SUNK	April 6, 1941
CAUSE OF SINKING	Scuttled
LOCATION	Dahlak Kebir, Eritrea
DISTANCE FROM SHORE	1 mile / 1,6 Km
MINIMUM DEPTH	16 ft / 5 m
MAXIMUM DEPTH	128 ft / 39 m
LENGTH	About 446 ft / 136 m

The Dahlak Islands archipelago lies in the southernmost part of the Red Sea, off the coast of Eritrea. The wrecks that lie in their waters date back to World War II.

When Italy entered the war in 1940, many Italian ships were docked in the ports and bays of Eritrea, which were part of the territory of what was then Italian East Africa. Before Eritrea fell into the hands of the British, the order was given to scuttle the ships, rendering them useless, while the crews were to give themselves up as prisoners of war.

In all, along the coasts of Eritrea, 33 small support boats and 25 cargo ships, tankers and troop transports were scuttled.

Most of them were later salvaged and reused by the British Navy, while three great Italian ships still lie underwater near the Dahlak Islands.

All traces of the *Giove* (scuttled on April 4, 1941) have been lost, while the other two are in Gubbet Muss Nefit, the great inland sea of Dahlak Kebir, the largest island in the archipelago, and their position is known.

The *Urania* (scuttled during the night of April 3-4, 1941) is easy to identify because parts of the hull break the water's surface, mingled with the wreck of a small Eritrean vedette that sank when it hit the ship.

The other, the *Nazario Sauro*, which sank on April 6, 1941, is a sort of Arabian phoenix that periodically appears and disappears. The first to find her again was Jacques-Yves Cousteau during one of his cruises in the 1950s. It was an easy task for the great explorer, because the ship's mast was still sticking out of the water. Cousteau, who did not know what ship it was, aptly nicknamed it the "the white-haired wreck," because the ship is covered with the long white stalks of whip corals.

Later on, the top of the *Nazario Sauro*'s mast broke off, came off, but today, thanks to modern GPS, the ship's position is known, and she is visited by the few cruise boats that manage to navigate this area between one ongoing war and another.

The ship lies upright on a sea floor about 128 ft (39 m) deep. At 446 ft (136 m) long, she requires more than one dive for a complete visit, and also because visibility is never excellent, even under the best conditions never more than 33 ft (10 m). The aft mast, where you begin your descent, rises 16 ft (5 m) from the surface, and the hull slowly begins to appear in the distinctively green water.

The rudder is still in position, while the propellers have been removed. Along the after portion, many parts of the rail are still standing, with sea squirts, sponges, hydro-zoans and long whip corals grasping everywhere. Swarms of fish hover around the deck, with the occasional jack passing through. Swimming to the deck, at a depth of about 82 ft (25 m), you'll find the ship almost completely intact, with the lifeboat supports still in place and the cargo windlasses perfectly discernible. The air intakes are still standing and

170 bottom
The Nazario Sauro *changed shipping companies and exterior appearance many times. In this period photo, we can see the stars on the smokestack that indicate her original ownership by the Società Transatlantica Italiana.*

171 top *These drawings show the ship as it changed color during the various periods of its life: red and black when it was launched; black and white after 1935, when the ship was owned by Tirrenia, with the disappearance of the stars on the smoke-stack, and white and yellow after 1938 under Lloyd Triestino.*

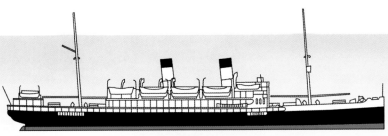

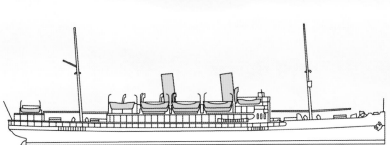

16 ft / 5 m

128 ft / 39 m

everywhere the ship is covered with a wide variety of life forms.

On the deck, a large sea anemone hosts numerous clownfish. The color of the water, the almost perfect conditions of the ship and the stalks of the whip corals give this dive a distinctive fascination. The sensation of discovery, the feeling of uncovering a mystery, pervades everywhere.

As you descend onto the foremast, you'll see that the starboard anchor is still in place, while the port anchor is on the sea floor, attached to the chain coming out of the hawsehole. The bow is vertical, entirely covered with whip corals. As you swim toward the stern, you'll see schools of barracudas, while on the deck there are various hatches leading to the holds. Windlasses and other loading equipment are in perfect condition. You'll then come to the bridge, where everything is in order.

If you're well-organized, you can visit many internal parts of the wreck, but even if you just wander through the outside areas, the ship is extremely fascinating. Going down the narrow corridors, you may also be surprised to find yourself face to face with an enormous barracuda, wondering which of you is more frightened by this unexpected encounter. From the cabin area, go to the stern mast. Looking up toward the surface, you'll be able to follow the ship's outline all the way to the end. Many fish are swimming about, including large angelfish, a big grouper and swarms of smaller fish. At the end of the mast, the top is covered with corals, sponges, sea squirts and a profusion of other encrusting organisms, while the water becomes more and more murky compared to the sea floor. As you surface, you'll feel that most of the mysteries of the *Nazario Sauro* are still concealed.

NAZARIO SAURO

172-173 A scuba diver with a flashlight, an indispensable tool especially in murky waters, observes the great bow windlass, where the large anchor chains are clearly visible and still in place.

173 top left The ship lies upright on the sea floor, with the vertical bow surrounded by the distinctively green water, caused by the wealth of plankton in the Gubbet Muss Nefit lagoon.

173 left center The ship is almost completely intact, and all the weapons on the deck are in perfect condition, covered with encrusting marine organisms.

173 bottom left In the center of the deck, below the bridge bulwark, there is a great sea anemone with its ever-present clownfish.

173 right The great trumpet-shaped ventilators on the deck are still in place, although the salt has corroded the thin plate in various areas.

"SHIPYARD"

BY CLAUDIO CANGINI

Local divemasters also call this diving area "Graveyard," although that may be an overly colorful expression for the two ships that lie here, neither of which sank as a result of war or claimed any victims.

The first wreck is the *Skipjack II*. She was the main cargo ship of the Felivaru Canning Factory, the only real industry in the Maldives archipelago. The factory, built here in the 1970s by a mixed Japanese-Maldivian company, still cans tuna. As faster and more efficient transportation systems took over, the 115 ft (35 m) long *Skipjack* became obsolete, and for several years she had been left anchored and unused in the inner lagoon at Felivaru Island. In 1985, the owners of the canning company decided to get rid of her and sink her in the open sea. When the managers of the Pro Diver diving center, based on Kuredu Island

just a few miles away it became aware of this, they offered to buy the ship in order to sink her near the resort and create a new diving area. Government authorities forbade this, and Pro Diver resigned itself to not having a wreck nearby.

But sometimes destiny has its own plans. Workers began to remove all structures of value from the *Skipjack,* and she was quickly emptied. A tugboat pulled up alongside the hull, whose end now seemed fated, and hooked onto one side to pull the ship away from the atoll, where her last voyage would end beneath the waves.

While the workers were using oxy-hydrogen flames to create a leak to facilitate the sinking, fire broke out and the flames immediately flared up. The *Skipjack* was abandoned, and to prevent the fire from spreading to the tugboat, the ropes that held her were cut. The accident occurred close to where the channel of the lagoon pass enters the ocean. The powerful current flowing in pushed the ship back, and she began to take on water from the stern.

Today the *Skipjack*'s stern is resting at the bottom of the pass, at a depth of about 98 ft (30 m), while the hull is resting on its starboard side on the wall of the channel. The rusty bow, which continued to burn for many days after the ship sank, remains at about 16 ft (5 m) above the surface.

The second wreck is 82 ft (25 m) long *Gaafaru*, which belonged to the same Felivaru cargo fleet. This ship, also unused, was intentionally sunk alongside the *Skipjack*. The *Gaafaru* remained in vertical position, with her stern on the sea floor and her

TECHNICAL CARD

TYPE OF WRECK	Cargo ships
NATIONALITY	Japanese
YEAR OF CONSTRUCTION	In the 1970s
DATE SUNK	1985
CAUSE OF SINKING	Scuttling
LOCATION	Lhaviyani Atoll, Maldives
DISTANCE FROM SHORE	Close to the reef wall
MINIMUM DEPTH	Skipjack II: at surface; Gaafaru: 66 ft / 20 m
MAXIMUM DEPTH	98 ft / 30 m
LENGTH	Skipjack II: 115 ft / 35 m; Gaafaru: 82 ft / 25 m

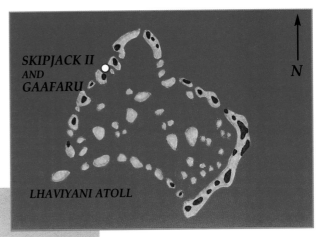

SKIPJACK II AND GAAFARU

N

LHAVIYANI ATOLL

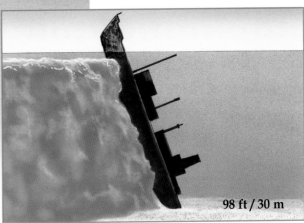

98 ft / 30 m

174 top The bow of the Skipjack II emerged 17 ft (5 m) above the surface. It's a good landmark to identify the place where the two ships sank.

174 bottom left A scuba diver approaches the bow of the Gaafaru. Until the fall of 1992, the wreck was positioned vertically, with the stern resting on the bottom and the keel on the wall. A violent storm pulled her to the floor, where she now lies on her port side.

175 top A boxfish (Ostracion cubicus) swims among the outside structures of the hull of the Skipjack II. The encrusting sponges and soft corals have completely cover every portion of the wreck.

"SHIPYARD"

keel wedged into the corals on the wall, until the fall of 1992, when a violent gale caused her to fall onto her port side on the sea floor. The two wrecks are a little over 100 ft (30 m) apart. Both cargo ships were of Japanese construction. So Pro Divers of Kuredu got one of the most fascinating diving areas of the Maldives for free.

"Shipyard" is on the west side of Lhaviyani (Faadhippolhu) Atoll. The two wrecks lie within the channel that separates the islands of Felivaru and Gaaverifaru, where the pass is about 100 ft (30 m) deep. In passes in the Maldives, the constant current to and from the open sea transports a large quantity of nutrients. This is one of the reasons why corals completely covered the two boats in such a short time. The encrusting hard and soft corals are dense and vigorous, and fish life is spectacular. Along the hull of the Skipjack, there

is a large school of batfish hovering with their snouts to the current. In the hold, you'll find numerous nurse sharks, which rest during the day. Meanwhile the entire range of colorful reef fish swim busily to and fro. Every cavity is filled with clouds of glassfish moving in silvery flashes. There are numerous large morays living in the crevices of this artificial branch of the reef. As in all passes, you may also see large, deep sea fish — reef sharks, tunas, and eagle rays.

The dive is best done with a slight current entering the atoll. Jump into the water just before the keel of the Skipjack, go beyond and take shelter behind the structure. Here, if there's no current, you can explore the entire deck, and then, pushed by the current, you'll come to the bow of the Gaafaru and can explore her entire length. On the sea floor between the two you'll find large

pieces of metallic structures that offer shelter to butterfly fish and groups of surgeonfish. The two wrecks are fine dives, and it's relatively easy to enter the hulls of both ships.

PACIFIC

BY EGIDIO TRAINITO

T alking about wrecks in the Pacific Ocean tends to become something of a war bulletin: the coasts of three continents, Asia, Australia and America, and the galaxy of archipelagoes and islands scattered across this ocean, were in fact a stage for the bloodiest war that has ever wracked the planet. Between the Japanese fighter-plane squadrons' attack on the American fleet at Pearl Harbor, Hawaii, and atomic bombs on Hiroshima and Nagasaki, a series of bloody attacks and counterattacks opened up an incredible number of fronts involving many archipelagoes in the Pacific.

Who would have thought in February 1944 that the destruction of the Japanese fleet in Micronesia, moored in the Truk Lagoon, would fifty years later become a tourist attraction for scuba-diving enthusiasts from all over the world, essentially changing the economy of that little archipelago? On those two dramatic days, 39 Japanese ships and 270 airplanes were lost with everything they carried, and many are still there underwater, barely covered by marine organisms and a layer of sediment and rust. The same holds for every other zone where the great campaigns of the war in the Pacific took place. Of necessity, this book includes only a limited number of wrecks, which nevertheless are a good representation of the extraordinary variety of vehicles that ended up on the sea floor. In Rabaul and other locations, there are landing vehicles and even tanks underwater, testifying to the enormous use of land troops throughout the conflict.

In contrast to such a wide distribution and variety of World War II wrecks, the non-military wrecks in the Pacific visited by scuba divers can be counted on two hands.

No trace remains of the event that allowed man to expand to all the islands scattered at such mind-boggling distances across the great ocean: because the crossings were made in small timber-built ships boats and nothing remains of their wrecks, which undoubtedly occurred. There are also very few traces of the 17th-century shipping traffic of the

OCEAN

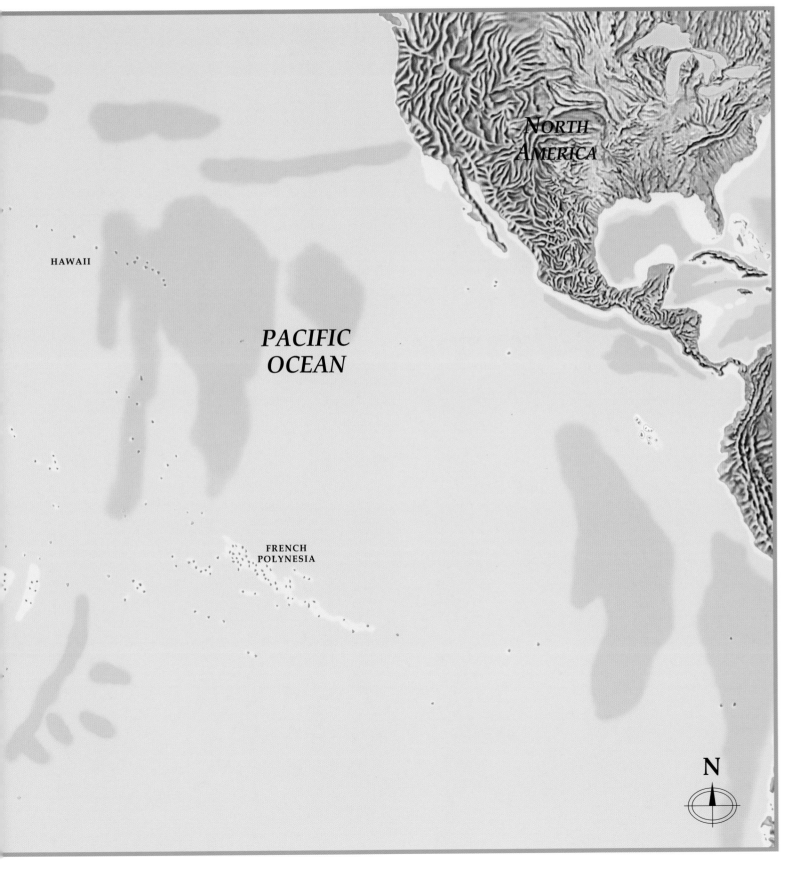

NORTH
AMERICA

PACIFIC
OCEAN

HAWAII

FRENCH
POLYNESIA

N

1) SHINKOKU MARU
2) AIKOKU MARU
3) SAN FRANCISCO
MARU
4) FUJIKAWA MARU
5) SANKISAN MARU
6) MITSUBISHI F1 M2
7) MITSUBISHI A6 M2
8) TOA MARU
9) GRUMMAN F6 F3
10) B-17 E
11) SS YONGALA

PACIFIC OCEAN

Dutch East India Company and the England's East India Company. We know of many shipwrecks along the western coast of Australia (the most famous is the wreck of the *Batavia*, which occurred in 1629, most of which was salvaged between 1963 and 1979), but the only wreck in the Pacific is the Dutch *Geldermalsen*, which was discovered in Indonesia but has not yet been explored. History may help us to understand why scuba-diving fans have so few wrecks to explore in the Pacific other than those from World War II. The western coast of Australia, New Zealand and Tahiti were explored for the first time by James Cook almost three centuries after the discovery of America. Moreover, construction of large North American ports on the Pacific coast is relatively recent, and only dates back as far as the early 20th century. The Pacific is an immense ocean, 70% larger than the Atlantic and two and a half times the size of the Indian Ocean, but modern navigation on it began only comparatively recently.

Dives on Pacific wrecks are often difficult. This is not due to temperature, because except for the southernmost areas like Tasmania, they are located in tropical environments where the temperature fluctuates from 20° to 28° C (68° to 82° F). But currents here are often powerful, wrecks may lie at depths greater than 30 meters, and in some cases, such as the Truk Lagoon, visibility rarely exceeds 33 ft (10 m)even under the best conditions. On the other hand, the most popular areas described in this book are served by well-organized tourist structures.

180-181 A diver uses his flashlight to illuminate one of the cannons on the Hakkai Maru, one of the warships sunk near the end of World War II in Rabaul bay.

181 One of the radial engines from an American Catalina seaplane that crashed during World War II lies on the sandy floor of Kavieng, Papua New Guinea.

TRUK LAGOON

BY VINCENZO PAOLILLO

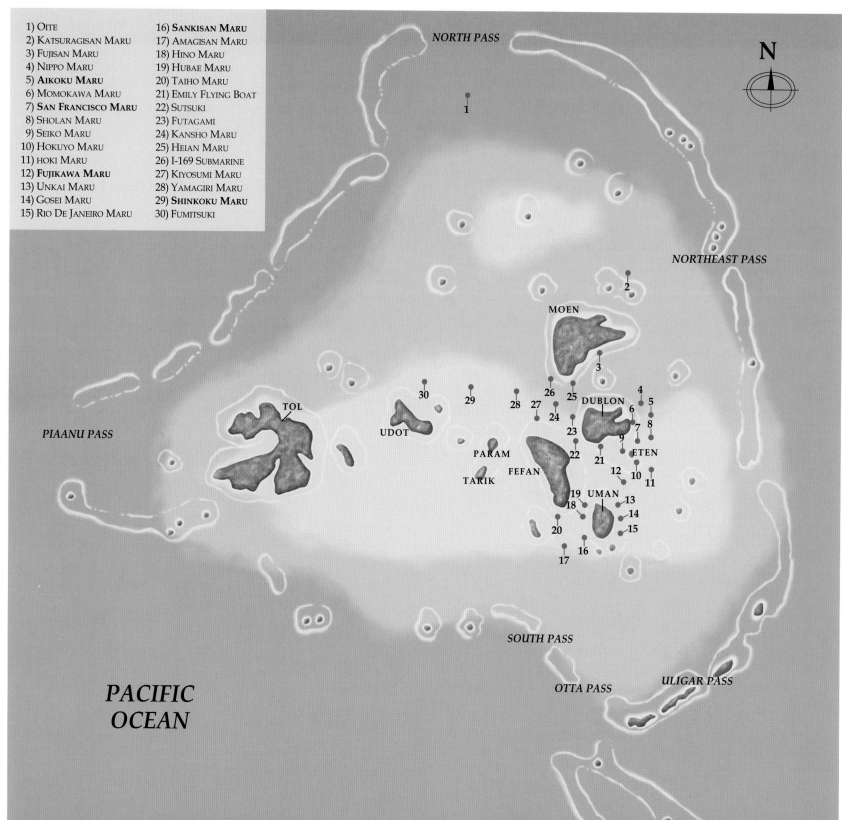

1) OITE
2) KATSURAGISAN MARU
3) FUJISAN MARU
4) NIPPO MARU
5) **AIKOKU MARU**
6) MOMOKAWA MARU
7) **SAN FRANCISCO MARU**
8) SHOLAN MARU
9) SEIKO MARU
10) HOKUYO MARU
11) HOKI MARU
12) **FUJIKAWA MARU**
13) UNKAI MARU
14) GOSEI MARU
15) RIO DE JANEIRO MARU
16) **SANKISAN MARU**
17) AMAGISAN MARU
18) HINO MARU
19) HUBAE MARU
20) TAIHO MARU
21) EMILY FLYING BOAT
22) SUTSUKI
23) FUTAGAMI
24) KANSHO MARU
25) HEIAN MARU
26) I-169 SUBMARINE
27) KIYOSUMI MARU
28) YAMAGIRI MARU
29) **SHINKOKU MARU**
30) FUMITSUKI

NORTH PASS

N

NORTHEAST PASS

MOEN

DUBLON

TOL

PIAANU PASS

UDOT

PARAM

FEFAN

TARIK

ETEN

UMAN

SOUTH PASS

OTTA PASS

ULIGAR PASS

PACIFIC
OCEAN

182 top Truk Lagoon is one of the largest in the world; it contains about a dozen volcanic islands that reach an elevation of 1640 ft (500 m), plus a myriad of smaller islets. The sea floor is less than 328 ft (100 m) deep, but for the most part the depth is shallower.

183 top Truk Lagoon in Micronesia has an extraordinary quantity of wrecks from World War II. In 1944, 39 Japanese ships and 270 Japanese airplanes were sunk by American bomber and fighter raids.

183 center and bottom The entire lagoon is scattered with the wrecks of small boats, landing vessels, pieces of airplanes, and military structures. Many break the water's surface, as the sea is quite shallow, and over the years have

formed disquieting, rust-colored war memorials. This is the case of the landing ship in the center and the cannon below, pointing out to sea on one of the many beaches on Moen, the island that is now the administrative center of Truk.

T ruk is a marvelous coral lagoon in the middle of the Pacific Ocean, east of the international date line and halfway between the Tropic of Cancer and the equator. At 825 sq. miles (2,130 sq. km), it's one of the largest lagoons in the world, with a coral perimeter of 140 miles (225 km) interrupted by only 5 navigable passes. Within it are about ten volcanic islands that reach a height of 1,640 ft (500 m), and a myriad of islets. The sea floor is not quite 328 ft (100 m) deep, but most areas are shallower than this. It was a highly strategic place during World War II, both because of its location halfway between Japan and New Guinea, the Solomons and the Bismarck archipelago, and because of its conformation. It was simple to block access by mining the passes, almost impossible to navigate among the emerging reefs and islets within it without highly detailed and completely up-to-date maps, and impossible to launch a

cannon attack from the outside against anyone in the middle of the lagoon.

The Japanese obtained Truk from their German allies at the start of World War I, and went to great lengths to keep it after the peace through a mandate from the League of Nations, then immediately fortified it in every way possible. Once World War II began, it became the most important base for their fleet. This is where the *Yamato*, the *Musashi* and other major aircraft carriers and battleships left for their missions. Allied commanders had considered an air attack on Truk since January

1942. However, after careful reconnaissance by the Australians, the failure of a first mission (happily without a great expenditure of forces) convinced them to put it off.

Then in February 1944, as the Allies were in the middle of their advance and after another reconnaissance mission revealed the presence of two squadrons with an aircraft carrier and a large battleship. The Allies decided to launch Operation Hailstone, a massive air attack led by a force that included 5 heavy and 4 light aircraft carriers.

The Japanese were aware of the situation, and only a few days prior

184 top Two divers
explore the imposing
side of the Rio de
Janeiro Maru,
which sank in the
waters southeast of
the island of Uman.

184 bottom left
A diver examines
the engine room
telegraph of the
Nippo Maru, now
completely
encrusted.

TRUK LAGOON

to the attack the Imperial Fleet commanded by Admiral Koga left the base, which was rightfully considered too exposed. Thus the massive Allied attack on February 16 and 17 found only 3 old destroyers, five oil tankers and about 30 transport ships, which were destroyed with about 300 airplanes, sacrificed in vain to defend them. The operation on Truk, which until then had been considered the Japanese Pearl Harbor, acted to neutralize the war-making capacity of this large atoll, making it unnecessary for American troops to invade it. Until the surrender in September 1945, the Allies thus limited themselves to periodic incursions to prevent the base from becoming any threat to them. For almost 25 years no one could touch the lagoon owing to the risk of setting off any of the thousands of unexploded bombs.

But today, after lengthy reclamation work, it has become a diving area with one of the highest concentrations of wrecks in the world. The shallow water of the atoll allows recreational divers to see no fewer than 40 ships, as well as various airplanes. With the exception of two destroyers and a few corvettes, they are mostly transport ships and large oil tankers, most of which are in good condition, with remarkable quantities of tropical life that have developed over the years. It's almost impossible to explore them all, but Truk certainly deserves a thorough visit.

184 bottom right Lanterns (in this case those of the Unkai Maru*) are one of the most common finds in the warships sunk near Truk.*

185 top left All wrecks at Truk are full of wartime equipment. Here we see gas masks, projectiles, and helmets from the Unkai Maru.

185 bottom left Gorgonians, alcyonarians, sponges, and corals completely cover the external structures of the Unkai Maru *at Truk.*

185 top right The Heian Maru *was a Japanese passenger ship converted to a support ship for submarines. Its name is clearly visible on the bow.*

185 right center The hold of the Hoki Maru *contains this truck covered with seabed organisms: the front part is almost completely intact.*

185 bottom right This well-preserved tank makes an exploration of the wreck of the Nippo Maru *especially fascinating.*

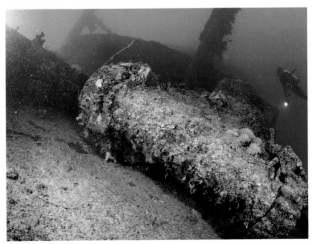

SHINKOKU MARU

BY ALBERTO VANZO

TECHNICAL CARD	
TYPE OF WRECK	Oil tanker
NATIONALITY	Japanese
YEAR OF CONSTRUCTION	1940
DATE SUNK	February 17, 1944
CAUSE OF SINKING	Bombing raid
LOCATION	Fefan Island, Truk Lagoon
DISTANCE FROM SHORE	About 1 mile / 1.6 km
MINIMUM DEPTH	40 ft / 12 m
MAXIMUM DEPTH	130 ft / 40 m
LENGTH	540 ft / 165 m

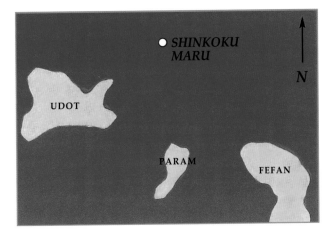

 Built in the Kobe shipyards in 1940 as an oil tanker, the *Shinkoku Maru* was assigned to provision the most important Japanese naval squadron, commanded by the legendary Admiral Yamamoto, who in the battle of Midway suffered the first great defeat of the war in the Pacific.

After escaping two submarine attacks, the *Shinkoku* arrived at Truk just a few days before the Allied offensive, and anchored northeast of the island of Fefan.

She miraculously avoided the first air attack, which began on the afternoon of February 16 from the aircraft carriers *Yorktown* and *Bunker Hill*. But her fate was sealed: the next morning she was sunk by another attack by torpedo bombers, and now rests on a seabed 40 meters deep.

Due to the *Shinkoku Maru*'s size, her masts rose above the water's surface for some time until they were demolished, as they created an obstacle to passing ships. Despite this, and although clearly visible from the surface when the water is clear, the wreck remained curiously unknown until 1971.

Today, along with the *Fujikawa Maru*, she is one of the easiest, best-known and most beautiful wrecks you can see in the lagoon.

The propeller is the deepest part of the wreck, while the superstructure and decks are between 26-49ft (8-15 m) deep, and the holds are no more than 115 ft (35 m) deep. But the ship is very large, over 492 ft (150 m) long and more than 66 ft (20 m) wide, so one dive is not enough to explore her in full.

The wreck is extremely colorful owing to the large number of corals and sponges, and is home to many reef fish. Schools of jacks and batfish often traverse the sea a little farther out. The most interesting areas are the superstructures to the back, where you'll find the smokestack, the deck with the bridge and the entire cabin area. The after cabins

occupy a large area, and on the floor you'll see, shaving razors with their cases that belonged to the crew.

On the port side near the engine room is a large gash caused by a torpedo, and above, on the deck, is an enormous three-legged trestle that was used for loading operations. On the poop deck is a cannon so heavily covered in corals that the muzzle is hardly recognizable.

The forward cabins are on the opposite side of the ship at a depth of 82 ft (25 m). Unfortunately discoveries of dishes, bottles and sake cups have become increasingly rare, although removing any objects is absolutely prohibited. Where the infirmary was once located, a collection of old 78 records still lies near a large number of medicine cruets, vials and syringes.

At the bottom of the forward cannon, which is also enveloped in an incredible variety of corals and alcyonarians, there are rounds of ammunition with unexploded projectiles, and a little farther off, two large lanterns that were once darkened with colored glass.

188-189 The ship was sunk during a torpedo attack, and the port side of the engine room has an enormous gash produced by a torpedo.

189 top left There are many large anemones at the base of the mainmast in the upper deck area leading to the quarterdeck.

SHINKOKU MARU

189 top right The wreck contains various objects that once belonged to crew members. Several old 78 records are still lying on the upper deck.

189 bottom On the forecastle, at a depth of 39 ft (12 m), are two large lanterns and the base of the cannon, as well as munitions with a number of unexploded projectiles.

AIKOKU MARU

BY ALBERTO VANZO

This was a 10,437-ton merchant ship built in 1939. She was used to transport passengers (about 400) and goods on behalf of an Osaka company. Her commercial use was brief, however, as in 1941 she was requisitioned by the Japanese admiralty and converted into an armed transport ship equipped with eight 5.5-inch guns, four torpedo launchers and machine guns, and two reconnaissance planes.

As her powerful engines could propel the *Aikoku Maru* at great speed, she was used for patrol activities. Her first known operation was the capture and subsequent torpedo sinking of the U.S. transport SS *Vincent* on December 12, 1941. Thereafter, she participated in many other operations that led to the capture and destruction of various Allied cargo ships until, on July 16, 1943, she was attacked by the submarine *Halibut*, which caused her quite serious damage. She was repaired and carried out numerous troop transport missions, then returned to Truk a few days before the Allied attack.

Hit by 500-lb bombs dropped by bombers from the aircraft carriers *Intrepid* and *Essex* between 8:15 and 8:30 on the morning of February 16, 1944, it exploded violently and sank almost instantly.

She now lies below about 195 ft (60 m) of water east of the island of Dublon, her forward section completely destroyed by the explosion, while the amidships and after sections are still in excellent condition.

The wreck was discovered by Jacques Cousteau's crew during their 1969 expedition, and he made

190 top The entire fore section of the ship was destroyed by the bombing, while the amidships and aft sections are well preserved at a depth of 195 ft (60 m).

190 top center The Aikoku Maru, *which was 492 ft (150 m) long, 66 ft (20 m) wide and about 39 ft (12 m) high, was originally a combined cargo*

and passenger ship. It had a draft of about 29 ft (9 m), and with its two massive 15,833-hp Mitsubishi engines could exceed 20 knots an hour.

190 bottom center and bottom This is what happened: on February 16, 1944, east of Dublon Island, American air forces attacked a Japanese convoy. The Reiyo Maru was hit, but the Aikoku Maru still seemed to be unscathed (top center of the photo). Then the Aikoku Maru (bottom center of the bottom image) was hit, and she sank in just a few minutes.

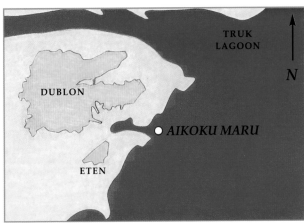

98 ft / 30 m

197 ft / 60 m

TECHNICAL CARD

TYPE OF WRECK	Cargo and passenger ship
NATIONALITY	Japanese
YEAR OF CONSTRUCTION	1939
DATE SUNK	February 16, 1944
CAUSE OF SINKING	Bombing raid
LOCATION	Dublon Island, Truk Lagoon
DISTANCE FROM SHORE	About 2 miles / 3.2 km
MINIMUM DEPTH	98 ft / 30 m
MAXIMUM DEPTH	197 ft / 60 m
LENGTH	525 ft / 160 m

a spectacular documentary about her. The *Aikoku* is one of the deepest and thus most challenging wrecks visited by scuba divers in the Truk lagoon, and it will take a number of dives to explore her completely.

A little less than 98 ft (30 m) deep is the smokestack, abundantly covered with corals and sponges, but the dive immediately becomes more difficult. The bridge is about 131 ft (40 m) down, the upper deck over 180 ft (55 m) deep, and the quarters below the bridge almost 164 ft (50 m) deep. You can see the area below through a rip in the starboard side of the first deck; a great caboose located in this part of the ship holds large ovens and sinks, with ceramic dishware, bottles and hot water containers scattered everywhere. You then enter the room that acted as a mess hall, where you will see the remains of numerous tables and their supporting frameworks.

Go toward the stern, and you

will see various structures, also colonized by a profusion of sponges, corals, gorgonians and splendid crinoids. You'll then come to the magnificent cannon set in its revolving base, still pointed skyward in firing position. In the second after deck, located below the gun deck and completing the steering equipment, is the base of the supplementary rudder, completely covered with a gaudy encrustation of sponges. When Cousteau's divers discovered the wreck, in the quarters below the deck they found the bodies of hundreds of sailors, or more likely soldiers, who evidently died during the explosion. Their bones were recovered by a Japanese delegation in 1984. They were partly buried and partly cremated according to the rituals of the Shinto religion, so that their souls could leave limbo.

On the same occasion, a commemorative plaque was placed on the deck in memory of all those who lost their lives in that tragic event. Evidently the recovery of these remains was not completed, because even today you can still find bones in various areas of the ship. This may be the last wreck at Truk where these macabre discoveries are still frequent.

193 top To complete the steering apparatus, the area below the cannon contains the base of the spare rudder, completely covered by encrusting sponges.

AIKOKU MARU

SAN FRANCISCO MARU

BY VINCENZO PAOLILLO

Not much is known of the history of this old cargo ship, built in 1919 in the Kawasaki shipyard in Kobe, requisitioned like many others by the Imperial Navy at the start of World War II, and first damaged by an Allied air attack in Wewak, New Guinea in May 1943.

The *San Francisco* arrived at Truk on February 5, 1944 with a large convoy, but remained when the other ships left on the 12th, along with the war fleet. Repeatedly attacked by bombers from the *Yorktown* and the *Essex*, and struck by numerous bombs that caused a huge fire, she sank on February 17, slipping slowly into the water stern first and coming to rest in an upright position.

She now lies over 230 ft (70 m) deep and is one of the most well-known and exciting dives on Truk. The ship is rather long, almost 394 ft (120 m), and lies in quite deep water. The bridge is 131 ft (40 m) deep, the platform of the aft cannon is 164 ft (50 m) deep, and the upper deck is over 180 ft (55 m) deep. This makes for a difficult dive, and you'll need

194 top The two tanks on the starboard side of the upper deck show clear traces of the fire that raged on board before the ship sank.

various trips to explore her completely. But you can see how fascinating she is in just one dive. In fact, locals refer to her as the "Million Dollar Wreck," both in reference to the large amounts of wartime materiel she holds and, according to others, because the remarkably clear water, unusual for Truk, makes the wreck extraordinarily beautiful.

The first structure you'll encounter as you descend is the mast, which is between holds nos. 1 and 2. You can then go on down to the bridge.

Here you can head right for the bow, where you'll see a fine light gun with the entire length of its bar-

rel covered by sponges and corals.

Going toward the stern, take a look at the hold, stuffed full of rows and rows of hemispherical beach mines and boxes of detonators. But it's better to stay on the upper deck to enjoy the most fascinating sight of the entire dive.

Here, between the entry to no. 2 hold and the bridge, on the port side of the ship, is a tank, apparently a model 97, called Chi-ha, heavily used by Japanese forces. It weighed 16 tons and was armed with a 7.7-mm cannon. The tank is still in excellent condition and almost looks ready for battle.

194 bottom This photograph shows the ship in 1937, when it was still unarmed.

TRUK
LAGOON

N

DUBLON

○ SAN FRANCISCO
MARU

ETEN

82 ft / 25 m

230 ft / 70 m

TECHNICAL CARD

TYPE OF WRECK	Cargo ship
NATIONALITY	Japanese
YEAR OF CONSTRUCTION	1919
DATE SUNK	February 17, 1944
CAUSE OF SINKING	Air strike
LOCATION	Dublon Island, Truk Lagoon
DISTANCE FROM SHORE	875 yds / 800 m
MINIMUM DEPTH	82 ft / 25 m
MAXIMUM DEPTH	230 ft / 70 m
LENGTH	384 ft / 117 m

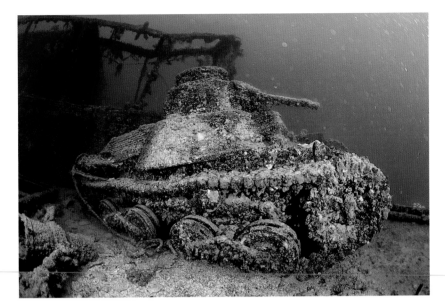

SAN FRANCISCO MARU

196 A diver swims above the bow of the ship, colonized by various corals and enormous sponges.

197 top left The tank on the port side of the upper deck, next to no. 2 hold, is covered with sponges but is still in excellent condition.

197 bottom left The cannon, mounted in a rotating position on the forecastle, is totally encrusted with red sponges and adorned with crinoids.

197 right The rear holds still contain neatly stowed engine parts, in particular racks with various torpedo casings.

On the other side of the upper deck are two more tanks, one of which rolled practically on top of the other as the ship sank.

These are a little more damaged. The armor of the first one has partially collapsed, and inside you can see the skeleton and engine. There are clear traces of the huge fire that struck the ship, but the tanks are still a thrilling sight.

The hatch to no. 2 hold is between the tanks. Inside you'll see two large fuel tankers with prominent tanks and enormous headlights.

All around are gas drums and bombs, probably airplane bombs.

You can then enter the bridge from the upper section: here the fire has destroyed almost everything, although the engine room telegraph is still is fine condition.

The back section is less interesting, and certainly the depth and the time spent in the front section will make an exploration impossible unless you make another dive.

On the upper deck, you'll see a thousand little things: bottles, containers of medicines, what remains of the smokestack, and then, in the rear holds, engine parts and racks with various torpedo casings.

Plates, glasses and bottles lie in the mud.

But the whole rear section seems seriously damaged, and everything bears traces of the fire.

FUJIKAWA MARU

BY VINCENZO PAOLILLO

T his 6938 ton ship was built in 1938 in the Tokyo ship-yards as a mixed passenger and cargo transport. She was requisitioned two years later by the Japanese navy and used as a transport ship for airplanes and railroad material. She performed tasks well first in Indochina, then in the Truk area, where on September 12, 1943 the *Fujikawa* suffered her first attack by a

U.S. submarine, which caused moderate damage. On the morning of February 16, 1944, not long afterbeing repaired, the *Fujikawa* has been attacked by numerous bombers. They did little damage. But she was attacked again that afternoon and was struck by a torpedo. Although badly damaged, the ship continued to float until the next day, when two Monterey VT planes delivered it the *coup de grâce* with torpedoes.

There was an enormous explosion as the ship was enveloped in flames. Shortly thereafter, she sank on a gently sloping sea floor 115-130 ft (35-40 m) below the surface.

The ship lies at a relatively shal-

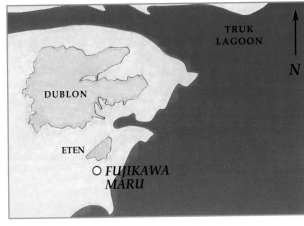

131 ft / 40 m

198 top A plaque commemorating the tragic events has been placed on Fujikawa's deck.

198 bottom The now uncovered deck structure is draped with splendid alcyonarians.

low depth. The bridge is only 49 ft (15 m) deep, the upper deck 65 ft (20 m), and the holds no more than 98-108 ft (30-33 m) below the surface. Not only is this one of the easiest dives on Truk, but it is also one of the most beautiful due to the incredible quantity of marine life that has formed on the ship and the significant number of sights waiting to be discovered.

As the ship is over 426 ft (130 m) long and there is a wide variety of things to see, you will make more than one dive. Normally divers descend along one of the two king-posts, one fore and the other aft; they are covered with an incredible quantity of soft corals in every color, sea fans, and branches of black coral.

The magnificent bow is totally encrusted with hard corals, branches of soft corals, and candelabra sponges, and the entire perimeter of the fore deck and its capstans are covered with a tangle of corals. In the center there is a fine cannon fes-

tooned with magnificent pink alcyonarians. Right behind the fore deck is the entrance to no. hold, where you will immediately see part of the load the *Fujikawa* was carrying: a torpedo tube, an engine, and most of all weapons, piles of rifles, and a myriad of cartridges and bullets scattered on the floor, as well as some airplane parts.

No. 2 hold is even more interesting. Here you will find more airplane

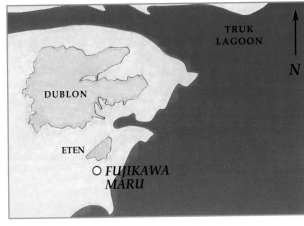

T E C H N I C A L C A R D	
TYPE OF WRECK	*Cargo ship*
NATIONALITY	*Japanese*
YEAR OF CONSTRUCTION	*1938*
DATE SUNK	*February 17, 1944*
CAUSE OF SINKING	*Air strike*
LOCATION	*Eten Island, Truk Lagoon*
DISTANCE FROM SHORE	*550 yds / 500 m*
MAXIMUM DEPTH	*131 ft / 40 m*
LENGTH	*433 ft / 132 m*

199 bottom The Fujikawa Maru, in the foreground to the left, still appears unharmed on the morning of February 16; at right, in the background the Tonan Maru is burning.

parts, including wings, fuselages, rudders, engines, and Japanese Zero undercarriages that have corroded into an incredible golden color. The bands of light entering from the openings make them even more spectacular. The hold is very large and well-lighted, the water clear, and even divers who suffer from claustrophobia will have no problems.

The magnificent amidships area contains the bridge with the smokestack and cabins.

The ceiling of the bridge has disappeared, leaving only the structures, which support an amazing quantity of red, pink, yellow and orange alcyonarians, accompanied by enormous crinoids that make the area look like a gaudy carnival celebration.

Enter through the engine room, where you'll see a complicated ventilation system designed to carry fresh air to the engine-room crew, or else go on toward the stern: outside is the usual explosion of colors, while inside the holds you'll see more tools, lanterns, gas masks, ceramic electrical materials, and bottles of sake. Right before the after mast is an anti-aircraft gun, and the deck holds another magnificent cannon that completed the ship's weaponry.

There are not many fish, although

200 top Beautiful candelabra sponges have grown on the bow; the silhouette of the cannon can be seen in the background.

200 bottom The engine room telegraph is recognizable here, magnificently encrusted with red sponges.

201 top A license plate, a cup and a dish are a few of the myriad objects in the holds of this ship.

201 bottom left A diver shows one of the numerous lanterns inside the hold.

201 bottom right Lanterns, gas masks, and electrical material cover the floor of the after hold.

you may see small groups of batfish, groupers, and scorpionfish, but if you look carefully, you'll see a riot of various kinds of nudibranchs moving across the upper deck.

If you like, descend along the starboard bulwark right behind the forecastle almost to the sand, where you'll see the great tear caused by the deadly torpedo blast that sank the

ship, or else enter the bridge to see the rooms, cabins and bathrooms located there.

One room is full of hundreds of bottles of "Dai Nippon Beer," while another one contains shoes, uniforms and inkpots. Some cabins have private latrines and one even has a private bathtub: truly exceptional luxuries for a transport ship of this period.

202-203 The upper part of the bridge has a spectral but extremely evocative atmosphere.

203 top left No. 2 hold is certainly the most interesting, as it is full of airplane spare parts.

FUJIKAWA MARU

203 center right In no. 1 hold , the cockpit of Zero fuselage is still intact.

203 bottom right The engine room, a detail of which is shown here, is accessible from the deck.

203 bottom left The tail of a Zero fuselage, still almost completely intact on the floor of no. 2 hold.

203 top right Pieces of fuselage, cockpits, wings, and rudders for Zero airplanes have taken on a golden color resulting from the action of corals and rust.

SANKISAN MARU

BY VINCENZO PAOLILLO

This ship has a very interesting history. Built in the United States in 1920 as a 4700-ton cargo ship almost 426 ft (130 m) long, she repeatedly changed names and owners until 1942, when, as the *Estero*, she was captured by the Japanese and used to transport wartime matériel, arms, airplane parts, tractors, munitions and so forth.

On February 16, 1944 the *Sankisan* was anchored close to the western shore of Uman Island in Truk Lagoon. She was attacked by a B17 bomber, which struck her with a 1000-lb bomb, and was machine-gunned by the fighters escorting it. She did not sink, and was attacked again the next morning, by a squadron of B-17s, one of which made a direct torpedo hit in the ship's after section, a little before the stern.

There was a terrible explosion that destroyed much of the bridge, the bul-

warks, and the after holds. The ship sank quickly, taking most of the crew with her. What remains of the stern now lies over 164 ft (50 m) deep and is connected to the bridge by a mass of metal of little interest to divers. This is the result of clean-up work done in 1974. To make the ship safe for divers, workers removed a powerful bomb they found in no. 1 hold, brought it to the rear section, and exploded it here.

The front central section of the ship lies in upright position on a seabed no more than 98 ft (30 m) deep.

The masts are about 16 ft (5 m) from the surface and the upper deck about 59 ft (18 m) down. This is one of the most colorful wrecks at Truk. Local guides say that owing to a particular pattern of currents, this is one of the best places to find alcyonarians, In fact, every structure, including the galleries, masts, capstans and derricks, is covered with enormous branches of soft corals in the most magnificent variety of colors: red, orange, yellow, and pink, scattered with soft corals, sponges and enormous sea shells. The

204 top It's the morning of February 17, 1944, and the ship has just been struck by a torpedo to starboard, while another one is one its way.

204 bottom The bow of the Sankisan *stands out in the blue waters of Truk Lagoon.*

TECHNICAL CARD	
TYPE OF WRECK	*Cargo ship*
NATIONALITY	*Japanese*
YEAR OF CONSTRUCTION	*1920*
DATE SUNK	*February 17, 1944*
CAUSE OF SINKING	*Air strike*
LOCATION	*Uman Island, Truk Lagoon*
DISTANCE FROM SHORE	*385 yds / 350 m*
MINIMUM DEPTH	*16 ft / 5 m*
MAXIMUM DEPTH	*98 ft / 30 m (stern, 164 ft / 50 m)*
LENGTH	*364 ft / 111 m*

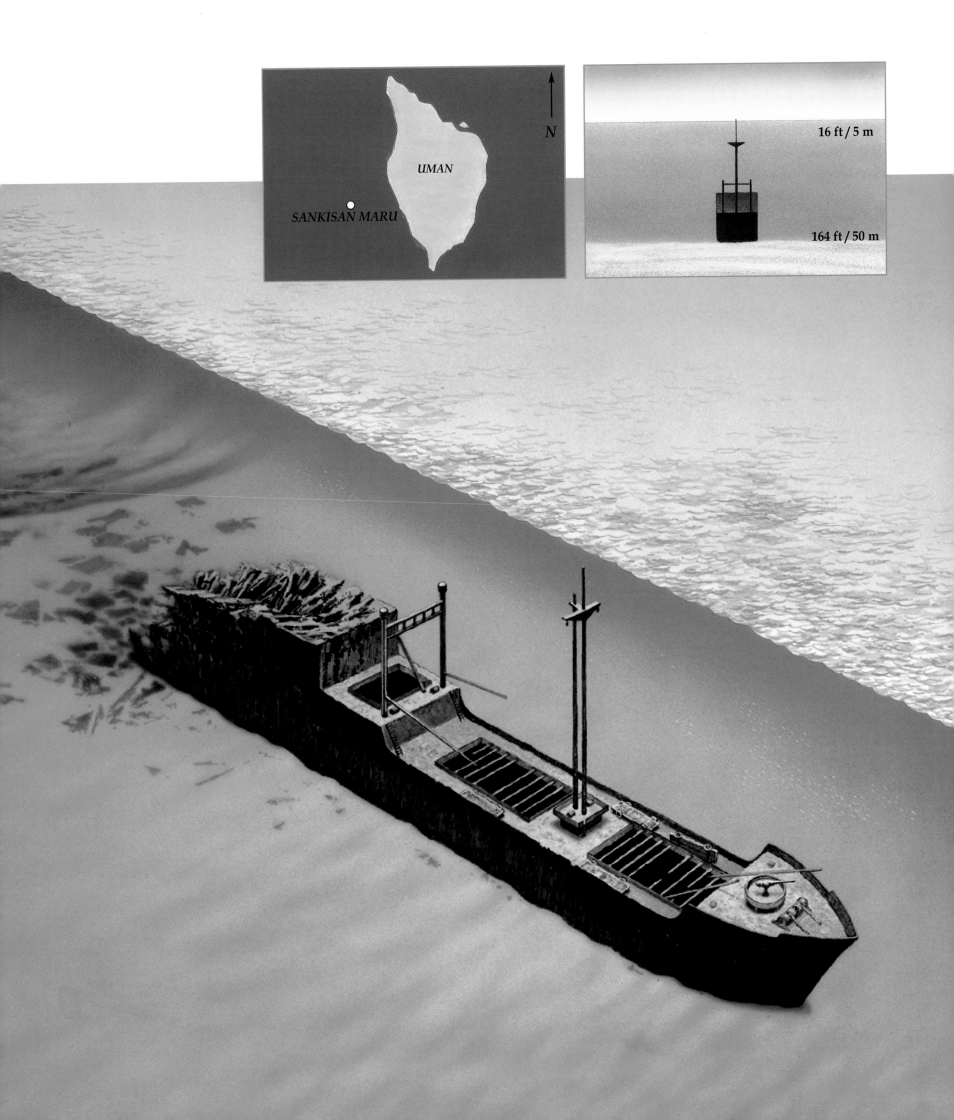

UMAN

SANKISAN MARU

N

16 ft / 5 m

164 ft / 50 m

bow, draped with gaudy beards of alcyonarians, stands out against the deep blue sea. The starboard hawse-hole still holds the chain of the anchor, which vanishes down in the sea. Right behind the foredeck, on the starboard side of the ship next to the opening to no. 1 hold, are the remains of two trucks, with just the structures, tires and steering wheel. In this hold are enormous quantities of munitions, grenades, and artillery shells, many in their containers, others scattered on the floor. During clean-up work, 284

depth charges were found, along with many artillery rounds.

After all these explosives were recovered, some were used to open up passages in the reefs of the lagoon to permit ships to sail through. No. 2 and 3 holds are connected. They contain munitions, airplane parts, engines, propeller blades, and on the upper levels, two trucks or at least parts of trucks, in only slightly better condition than those on the upper deck. Right before the end of the front section of the ship, on the two sides of the upper deck, are the machine-gun positions, on which someone has placed numerous cartridge clips.

206 left A steering wheel and loading platform are all that remain of one of the vehicles that was on the upper deck.

206 top right This cannon is still mounted on its rotating platform.

206 bottom right Soft corals, hard corals and alcyonarians embellish the structures of the Sankisan Maru.

206-207 Rich coral formations and alcyonarians have grown on the bow.

207 top A diver has placed some cartridge clips at the base of a machine gun on the upper deck of the Sankisan Maru.

208-209 This sort of cartridge belt is one of the most interesting finds in the hold.

209 top left Inside a hold, a diver uses his flashlight to illuminate a truck.

209 center left The front part of a small vehicle rests on the upper part of no. 2 hold.

209 top right Thousands of rusted machine gun projectiles cover the floor of the holds.

209 bottom The leaf spring, two wheels and little else indicate that a truck once stood in the lower part of no. 1 hold.

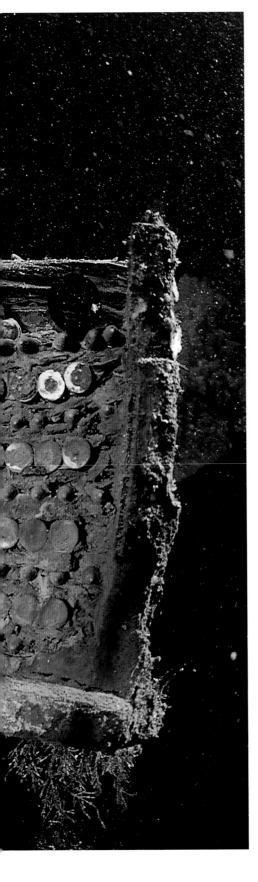

RABAUL BAY

BY VINCENZO PAOLILLO

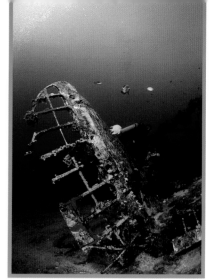

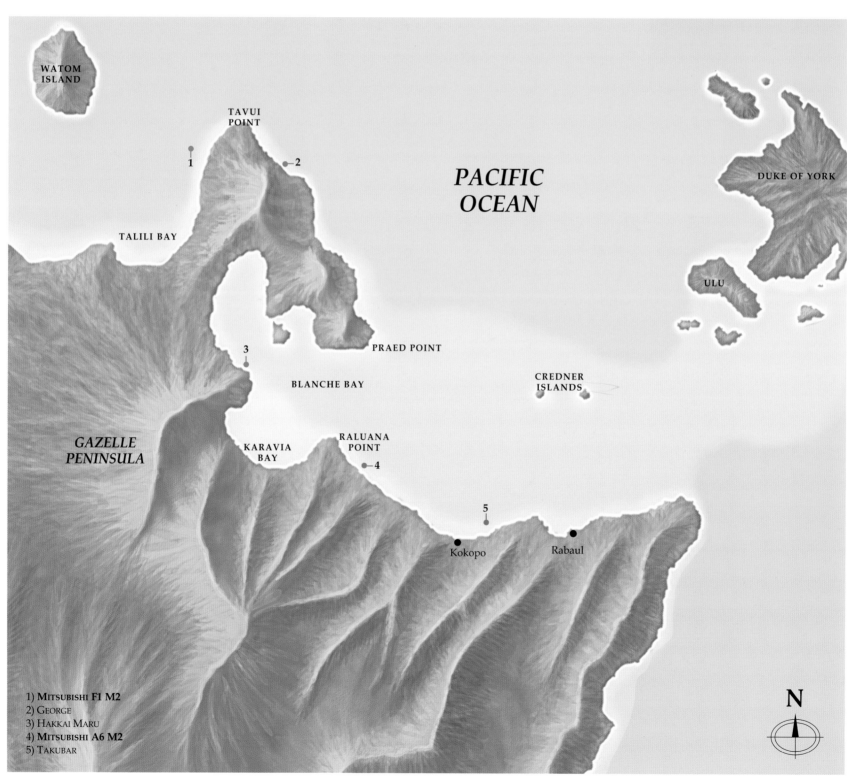

WATOM
ISLAND

TAVUI
POINT

1

2

TALILI BAY

PACIFIC
OCEAN

DUKE OF YORK

ULU

PRAED POINT

3

BLANCHE BAY

CREDNER
ISLANDS

GAZELLE
PENINSULA

KARAVIA
BAY

RALUANA
POINT

4

5

Kokopo

Rabaul

N

1) MITSUBISHI F1 M2
2) GEORGE
3) HAKKAI MARU
4) MITSUBISHI A6 M2
5) TAKUBAR

210 top This
Mitsubishi F1 M2
biplane, or "Pete," as
the Allies called it, is
in good condition.
The rudder has lost
its light structures,
but the supporting
structures remain,
with groupers and
seabream passing
through almost
playfully.

211 A diver explores
the deck of the
Hakkai Maru,
which sank at the
entry to Simpson
Harbor. The large
capstan is visible in
the foreground, while
the silhouette of a
cannon stands out in
the distance.

At 7:55 a.m. on December 7, 1941, Japanese torpedo bombers launched their attack on Pearl Harbor. This first part of the plan devised by Admiral Yamamoto was designed to make the Japanese armed forces masters of most of the Western Pacific in less than three months. But Yamamoto, who was actually against the war, understood that he had to get even farther, all the way to Australia, and do it even faster in order to anticipate the Allied reaction and force them to reach a satisfactory peace with the Land of the Rising Sun. So he needed a large base as close as possible to the lands to be conquered, where he could reprovision his fleet and from which squadrons of bombers could continue to pour out.

It didn't take long to see that the best place was Rabaul. It had a marvelous bay with a natural sheltered harbor where dozens and dozens of ships could hide, high mountains that would make an enemy air attack difficult, and flat areas where airports could be built.

So on January 22, even before the Australians, who had gotten wind of what was coming, could complete their evacuation, he began an attack that lasted less than 24 hours. The little garrison was destroyed, and the 400 civilians who remained were deported, later vanishing in the sea when the ship taking them to concentration camps was sunk (in an irony of fate, through one of the first successes by US submarines).

Along with their landing troops, Japanese and Korean engineers began construction of an incredible system of fortifications, block houses,

artillery positions, airports hidden in the jungle, and most importantly, hundreds of miles of tunnels that traversed the mountains, creating underground refuges and storehouses.

This is where Admiral Yamamoto made his headquarters, from which Japanese airplanes left to bomb New Guinea and Australia. And this is where the fleet took refuge to reprovision and depart again for its bold incursions.

But the wind soon changed, and Rabaul Bay was frequently the target of furious bombing raids by Allied planes. The city was once again devastated, the airports rendered useless, and hundred of airplanes were destroyed on the ground. But over 100,000 Japanese (and, for the record, over 1000 Korean prostitutes) continued to live in its burrows and tunnels, remaining there until the end of the war. The base operated almost solely by night, when ships arrived with materials or to reprovision. At night, support boats emerged from caves on rails hidden by vegetation and frenetically loaded or unloaded victuals and arms. Submarines emerged at night after lying submerged all day along the walls that in the north plunged down from a height of over 3000 ft (900 m).

By dawn everything stopped. The ships sailed away, the remaining airplanes took off, and the base's defenders retreated to the caves.

The system worked so well that even when the Japanese were in retreat throughout the Pacific, the Allies resisted any temptation to conquer Rabaul Bay, and limited themselves to neutralizing it by subjecting it to constant bombing. When the base surrendered at the end of the

war, it was so stuffed with arms and munitions that the only thing the Allied commander could do was to leave everything there and wall up all exits. Numerous wrecks lay in the bay on the bottom of the sea. There were transport ships, refrigerator ships, and boats sunk by Allied airplanes. Those in shallower waters were gutted by explosions and demolished right after the war, primarily for purposes of salvaging their iron. The boats that lay in deeper waters remained essentially intact, bringing joy to scuba divers.

But it didn't last long. Rabaul is surrounded by active volcanoes that have been subject to tremendous explosions over the years. On September 19, 1994, Tavurvur, a volcano that was right behind the airport,

exploded with an enormous roar, followed shortly by Vulcan on the other side of the bay. For days, not only lava but also an enormous quantity of pumice and ash covered the surrounding area. Rabaul was destroyed and everything that was there was covered with a thick shroud. For many years thereafter it was impossible to dive on the *Hakkai Maru*, the *Italy Maru*, the *Manko Maru*, the *Kensing* and the dozens of other ships lying here. Scuba diving has slowly returned, but visibility in the bay, where the current is weak, is quite limited, less than 50 ft (15 m).

It's better to try the wrecks on the outside that were farther away from the eruption and less affected by it: the *George*, the *Takubar,* and especially the two airplanes.

MITSUBISHI F1 M2

BY VINCENZO PAOLILLO

TECHNICAL CARD	
TYPE OF WRECK	Bomber
NATIONALITY	Japanese
YEAR OF CONSTRUCTION	1941/1942
DATE SUNK	Presumably 1942
CAUSE OF SINKING	Unknown
LOCATION	Rabaul, Papua New Guinea
DISTANCE FROM SHORE	230 ft / 70 m
MINIMUM DEPTH	75 ft / 23 m
MAXIMUM DEPTH	82 ft / 25 m
LENGTH	40 ft / 12 m

A beautiful airplane wreck lies no more than 328 ft (100 m) from the shore west of Tavui Point, the promontory that ends the Rabaul peninsula to the north. This Mitsubishi F1 M2, which the Allies commonly referred to as a "Pete", is a seaplane with a curious, seemingly antiquated structure, although production did not begin until 1936.

It's not a large plane, a little less than 39 ft (12 m) in length and wing span, and is equipped with a main pontoon and two small stabilizers below the wings. It could fly long distances and had a special ability to ascend to significant altitudes (over 32,800 ft / 10,000 m). This airplane was used for both reconnaissance and as a fighter and bomber.

It was an extremely practical plane: because of its small size, it could easily be housed on transport ships or battleships, from which it could be lowered into the sea by a crane and recovered in the same way at the end of the mission.

And the fact that this one apparently has no damage to the fuselage or the wings, with only its main pontoon broken, and has a rope attached, shows that it probably sank owing to a faulty maneuver

212 top Airmen on a Japanese base preparing a Mitsubishi for a mission.

212 bottom "Pete," as the Allies called this plane, is still perfectly preserved, despite the 60 years it has spent under water.

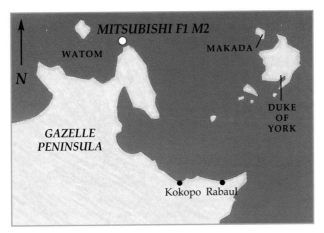

MITSUBISHI F1 M2

WATOM

MAKADA

DUKE
OF
YORK

GAZELLE
PENINSULA

Kokopo Rabaul

N

75 ft / 23 m

82 ft / 25 m

214-215 The upper wing and stays make a base for coral, alcyonarian coral, and feather stars and offer a refuge to groupers.

214 bottom The plane lies on the ocean's sandy bottom, gently reclining on its left side.

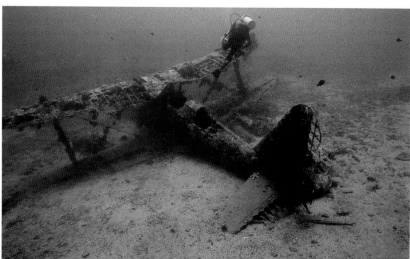

215 top left In the cockpit, part of the seat and the control panel are still visible.

215 top right On the fuselage, above cockpit, a machine-gun mounting can be glimpsed.

MITSUBISHI F1 M2

while it was being placed in the water or recovered from it by the support ship, perhaps during an enemy attack.

The "Pete" can be reached in a short swim from the beach, with just a few difficulties posed by the emerging reef, or by boat, and rests perfectly on a sandy seabed no more than 66-82 ft (20-25 m) deep, slightly sloping to the left.

Except for the clear damage to the main pontoon, which confirms our theory on why it sank, the airplane is almost completely intact, with all its structures covered with sponges, pink, mauve, yellow and orange soft corals, and white, black and yellow crinoids.

Its propeller with three blades is in perfect condition and is covered with encrusting sponges, and Moorish idols (*Zanclus cornutus*), damselfish, small butterflyfish, and soldierfish swim playfully around the panels of the tail rudder.

The wing's guide wires are now adorned by festoons of crinoids and sponges. The two seats (pilot and gunner) are almost completely intact, with the seats and control stick fully visible. Clouds of glassfish swim inside.

An exception is the radio, which lies a few meters away. This was evidently carried off by a scuba diver who either thought the better of his deed or was unable to carry the radio because of its weight.

The machine gun, however, is missing from where it should be in front of the back seat, and was evidently stolen some time in the past.

But there is a beautiful moray hiding under the right wing, as well as a profusion of little groupers moving slowly or hovering immobile below the fuselage and the roof of the wings, or scrutinizing divers from behind a propeller blade.

215 center The virtually intact propeller blades are now covered with encrusting sponges.

215 bottom Coral life has completely taken over the wing rods. A multitude of feather stars and several types of coral fish can be seen.

215

MITSUBISHI A6 M2

BY VINCENZO PAOLILLO

T he second beautiful airplane wreck in the Rabaul area is an example of what may be the most famous fighter plane of the entire Second World War, and certainly the greatest symbol of Japanese power.

The Mitsubishi A6 M2 was a very small plane (just a little over 29 ft / 9 m long with a wing span of 39 ft / 12 meters), made of ultra-light aluminum, with a powerful engine that allowed it to reach the truly exceptional speed for that time of 340 mph (565 kph). It had an even more incredible flying range of almost 1500 miles (2400 km) and was armed with two light cannons and two machine guns, but could also carry bombs.

This highly maneuverable airplane where everything, including the pilot's safety, was sacrificed to performance, had its glorious baptism by fire in the attack on Pearl Harbor, and also covered itself in glory during the less successful battle of Midway. Its features allowed it to keep up the pace for the entire war, not only with the better armed U.S.

TECHNICAL CARD

TYPE OF WRECK	Fighter plane
NATIONALITY	Japanese
YEAR OF CONSTRUCTION	1941/1942
DATE SUNK	Presumably 1942
CAUSE OF SINKING	Unknown
LOCATION	Kokopo, Rabaul
DISTANCE FROM SHORE	About 262 ft / 80 m
MINIMUM DEPTH	98 ft / 30 m
MAXIMUM DEPTH	98 ft / 30 m
LENGTH	29 ft / 9 m

powerful vehicles or airplanes that had less ability to flee the enemy, but only three, almost completely intact, have been found in shallow waters here. One was salvaged and sent to the aerospace museum in San Diego, California, while another went to the science museum in Tokyo. The third lies in about 30 meters of water a short distance from Kokopo beach 26 kilometers south of Rabaul, and can be visited by scuba divers.

It's a good swim from the beach, or you can use a boat and dive down on top of it. It lies on a sandy plateau, its right wing partially covered by mud, with the left one slightly raised from the sea bed.

The plane has a row of bullet

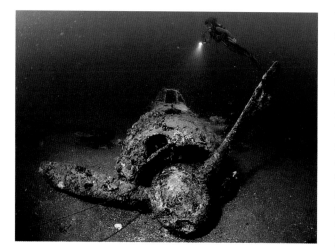

Wildcat aircraft, but also with the more powerful Hellcat that the Americans built especially to deal with the difficulties A6 M2 posed. Over 10,000 of these planes were built after 1940, but certainly very few remained by the end of the war. Yet the success they achieved throughout the Pacific campaign, especially during the first part, when the Allies had not yet found the appropriate countermeasures, was truly exceptional. Hundreds of them were destroyed in the battle of Rabaul, sacrificed to protect more

holes along the fuselage running from the area where the pilot's legs were all the way to the engine, which leads one to believe that the engine had died by the time of impact. This prevented two propeller blades from breaking, while the third one has now disappeared.

The airplane's small size, its position perfectly upright in the sea floor, and the relatively shallow depth, permit a tranquil, thorough, detailed exploration. The two remaining propeller bladesare covered with beautiful encrusting

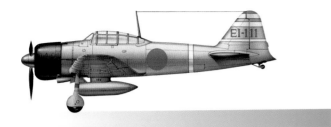

216 top and 217 top
Seen from the front
and the side, the Zero
displays its powerful,
aggressive lines.

216 center left
On the deck of an
aircraft carrier, airmen
finish arming a Zero
squadron about to
leave on a mission.

216 center right The
photo depicts a Zero
on a mission above
the waters of the
Pacific.

216 bottom
The propeller lost one
of its blades on impact
with the water. The
other two are covered
by encrustations.

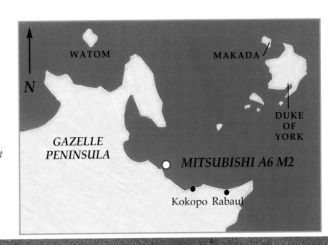

N

WATOM

MAKADA

GAZELLE
PENINSULA

DUKE
OF
YORK

MITSUBISHI A6 M2

Kokopo Rabaul

98 ft / 30 m

sponges and fire coral; the fuselage is totally encrusted with corals, sponges, and little gorgonians; the cockpit is full of glassfish; and a large soft coral has grown on the back of the pilot's seat.

The control panel is still clearly visible. The tail and rudder are magnificent, and a profusion of hydroids has grown on the rudder's grid.

Hard corals have grown on the wings, along with some beautiful leather corals. There are many fish all around: small red groupers, damselfish and small schools of snappers (*Lutjanidae*), while morays and lobsters have been found under the wings.

Little is known how the plane ended up here. According to the Tolai (the local population that lives in the Rabaul area), one unspecified day the plane crashed into the water, and the pilot emerged, swam to shore and disappeared. Rabaul was in Japanese hands at that time.

218 top left
The cockpit serves as a refuge for a flurry of glass fish.

218 top right
Gorgonians and hydroids have taken possession of the rudder frame.

218 bottom
Sponges and
madrepores of
varying shapes have
entirely colonized
the airplane's frame.

218-219 Mitsubishi
lies on the sandy
bottom that has
partially covered some
of its right wing.

SOLOMON ISLANDS

BY VINCENZO PAOLILLO

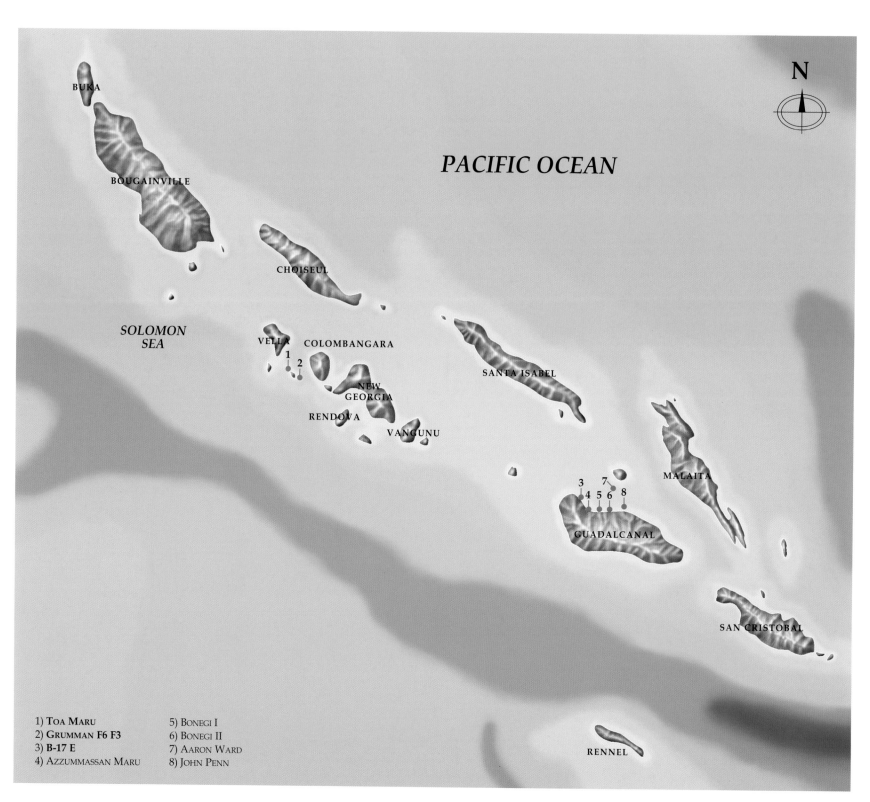

N

PACIFIC OCEAN

BUKA

BOUGAINVILLE

CHOISEUL

SOLOMON
SEA

VELLA   COLOMBANGARA

1
2

NEW
GEORGIA

RENDOVA

VANGUNU

SANTA ISABEL

MALAITA

3   7
4 5 6 8

GUADALCANAL

SAN CRISTOBAL

RENNEL

1) **Toa Maru**
2) **Grumman F6 F3**
3) **B-17 E**
4) Azzummassan Maru

5) Bonegi I
6) Bonegi II
7) Aaron Ward
8) John Penn

The Japanese navy's February 1943 evacuation of about 11,000 exhausted, hungry, and wounded Japanese soldiers afflicted by a variety of diseases, was not only a significant strategic defeat, but also marked a decisive turning point in the war in the Pacific. The Japanese saved about 11,000 men (many in such poor condition that they were incapable of fighting again for many months, if ever), but they left over 26,000 men killed in combat or by disease, compared to 2000 for the Allies. They lost 800 airplanes and 2000 pilots compared to less than 250 for the Allies, and above all had to abandon a base crucial to the outcome of the war. Thereafter, they never again waged an offensive war, but were always on the defensive. The Guadalcanal campaign began in early 1942, when the Japanese occupied all the Solomon Islands and started to build a large airport. The intention was clear: a huge new base in addition to Rabaul, which they had recently occupied, that could be used to launch a conquest of the entire South Central Pacific, perhaps as far as Australia and New Zealand. The danger could have been mortal, and the Allies rushed to remedy the situation with a major landing in early 1942.

The Japanese at first lost ground and then abandoned the area where they had been building the airport. The Americans took it over, naming it after a marine who had distinguished himself in the battle of Midway. It became the legendary Henderson Field (today it's the Henderson Field Airport of Honiara, the new capital of the Solomon Islands). But then began what would become the longest, most intense, violent and cruel campaign of the entire war. For over 6 months, the

Allies and the Japanese battled back and forth in an endless series of attacks and counter-attacks that included Japanese suicide battalions, in an incredible slaughter. At the same time, fighter planes battled in the air, suffering terrible losses, and naval fleets fought by sea. Six of the most important naval battles in the entire war were fought here, with shifting results and brutal costs on both sides. Large numbers of aircraft carriers, battleships, cruisers, and submarines were destroyed and their crews lost. About 50 warships lie submerged in the only channel that separates the of Guadalcanal Island from Nggela Island, with an even greater number of transport ships, cargo ships, and oil tankers from both sides, so that today the straits are known as "Iron Bottom Sound."

Most of these wrecks lie too deep for recreational divers, while others have been reduced to masses of wreckage that are of no interest. Some exceptions include two Japanese transport ships stranded across from Honiara and identified by the name of the place (Bonegi I and Bonegi II), a large American troop transport ship, the *John Penn*, which lies right across from the airport, another Japanese transport ship, the *Azzummassan Maru*, which is sunk perpendicular to the beach at Ruaniu, a Japanese submarine, an American Flying Fortress, and on the opposite side of the straits, lying in deep water (from 184-246 ft / 56-75 m below the surface), an American destroyer, the *Aaron Ward*. But wrecks abound throughout the Solomons. Most of them are totally destroyed, but some still offer thrilling sights.

A short way away is the Japanese cargo ship *Toa Maru* and a little farther away an American airplane, the Hellcat. They have the honor of being near a small island known as Plum Pud-

ding, or Vasolo Island, that is no more than 324 ft (100 m) in diameter and covered with dense vegetation. The island gained fame because a certain John Fitzgerald Kennedy, a few decades before becoming one of the most famous presidents of the United States, found refuge there with a some of his men, as commander of an American motor torpedo boat, the PT-109, which was sunk by the Japanese.

221 The true name of the wreck known as the Bonegi 2 *was the* Kinugawa Maru, *a Japanese cargo ship sunk by American artillery off the coast of Honiara. This photo shows a portion of the encrusted deck, along with a circular platform, perhaps the base of a capstan.*

TOA MARU

BY VINCENZO PAOLILLO

This 6732 ton transport ship was over 460 ft (140 m) long, and carried both passengers and cargo. She was first launched in late 1938, at Osaka.

After serving briefly as a merchant ship, she was requisitioned in 1941 by the Japanese navy and used to transport wartime materiel.

In January 1943, the *Toa Maru* was assigned to transport provisions, munitions and arms from New Georgia to Vila Harbor, the departure base for the so-called Tokyo Express, the convoys of fast Japanese boats (destroyers, cruisers, etc.) that sought to bring provisions to Japanese troops defending Guadalcanal, traveling quickly at night in order to avoid Allied air attacks.

As she made the trip, she was sighted by Australian reconnaissance, who signaled her presence to the Allied command at Guadalcanal. From an aircraft carrier operating in the area, the Allies sent a squadron of 12 Dauntless dive bombers escorted by 8 Grumman F4 Wildcat fighters.

As the *Toa Maru* was escorted by a squadron of Zeros and float planes, an air and naval battle ensured. The commander of one of the two squadrons of Wildcats, Lieutenant Jefferson J. De Blanc, covered himself with glory by downing 2 float planes and 3 Zeros, until he too was shot down. De Blanc managed to parachute out but had to swim for 6 hours before he reached the shore, where he was aided by the locals, who hid him from the Japanese. After two weeks of misadventures, he was finally rescued by Allied coast watchers and reached Guadalcanal; four years later he received the Congressional Medal of Honor. In the meantime, the *Toa Maru* had suffered various attacks from bombers, whose crews did not believe they had hit the ship. But a bomb had in fact struck her forecastle, seemingly without a trace, yet actually causing an enormous internal fire that the crew was unable to control.

The commander flooded the fore holds, but was only able to save that part of the ship, and could not stop the fire that was spreading toward the stern. At this point, the only thing he could do was head for Gizo Island, and there, in the shallow waters of Koluku Bay, the *Toa Maru*

222 top *The size of the ship's stern is truly awe-inspiring compared to the figure of the diver to the right, lies 125 ft (38 m) deep.*

222 bottom *The ship lies on her side so that her door now looks like an escape hatch.*

223 center *In the drawing above the* Toa Maru *is seen reversed, on her starboard side. Below, the ship is seen in a cross-section.*

TECHNICAL CARD

TYPE OF WRECK	*Cargo ship*
NATIONALITY	*Japanese*
YEAR OF CONSTRUCTION	*1938*
DATE SUNK	*January 31, 1943*
CAUSE OF SINKING	*Air strike*
LOCATION	*Koluku Bay, Gizo Island, Solomon Islands*
DISTANCE FROM SHORE	*324 ft / 50 m*
MINIMUM DEPTH	*26 ft / 8 m*
MAXIMUM DEPTH	*125 ft / 38 m*
LENGTH	*443 ft / 135 m*

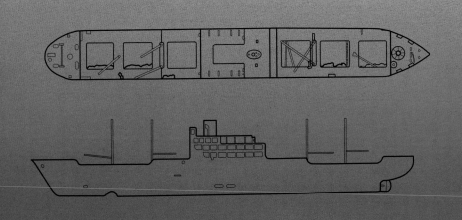

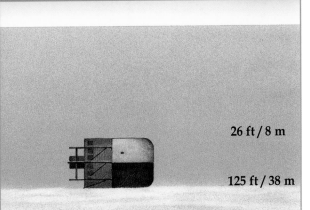

26 ft / 8 m

125 ft / 38 m

TOA MARU

224 The profile of
the Toa Maru's
bow appears in the
waters of the
Guadalcanal.

225 top left
Numerous bottles of
sake are still found
in the hold.

225 top right
A pistol was found
between the bottles
of sake and beer.

225 bottom left
The stern mast's
frame is covered by
encrusting sponges
and corals.

225 bottom right
The rails have been
attacked by algae
and coral, forming
eerie metal
sculptures.

sank, coming to rest on its starboard side.

The crew members who did not perish in the battle or the enormous fire were easily able to reach the shore and save themselves. The dive is not especially difficult: the bow rests only 26 ft (8 m) deep, and the stern about 125 ft (38 m) below the surface. There are very visible traces of the fire on the bridge, the structures, and nos. 4, 5 and 6 holds, where glass, silverware and utensils are a solidified mass.

The anti-aircraft gun that was on the upper deck is lying in the sand right next to the stern. If you go up along the hull, you can explore the six holds, where everything there that has not been carried off is piled on the right side, which is now the floor, or spilled out onto the sand. You'll find bottles of beer and sake, utensils and munitions, machine gun clips, rifles, which now look like a mass of corals, and several pistols. A sidecar, tractors, trucks and even a small tank are mostly lying in the sand along the side of the ship, everything in the middle of sponges, alcyonarians and branches of black coral. There are not many fish, although inside the dark hold there are some small schools of snappers. It's easy to spot large scorpionfish and flatheads below the bow. Locals say that sharks often come here, but we never saw one.

GRUMMAN F6 F3

BY ALBERTO VANZO

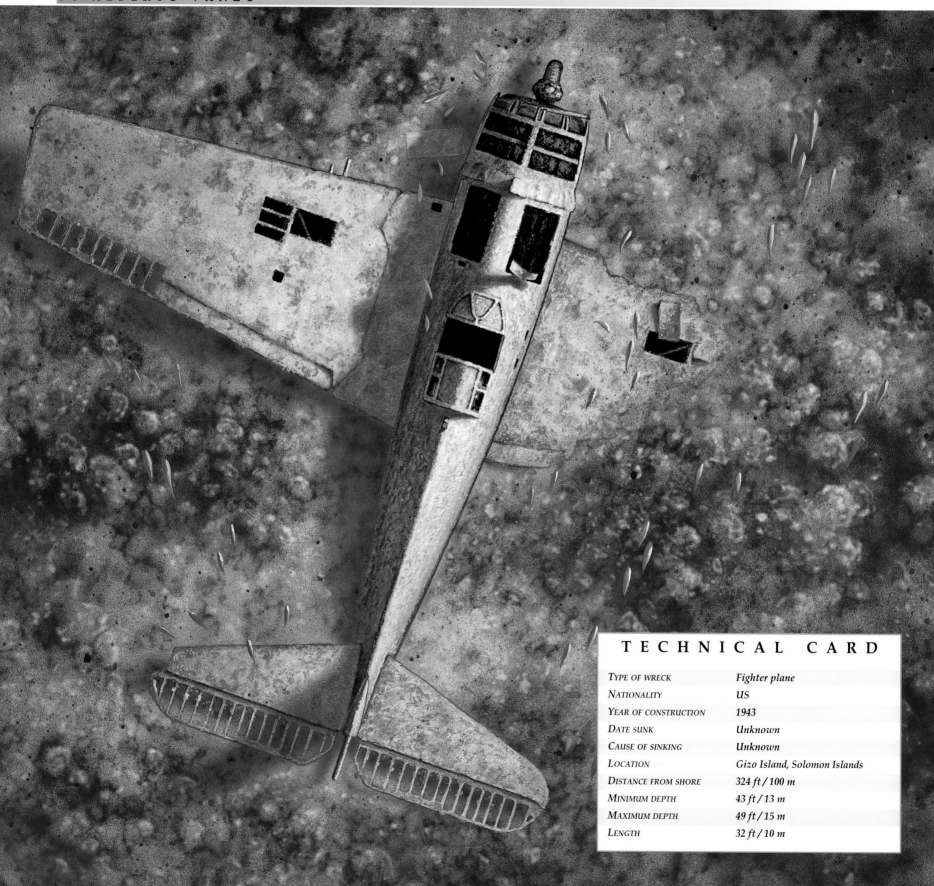

TECHNICAL CARD

TYPE OF WRECK	Fighter plane
NATIONALITY	US
YEAR OF CONSTRUCTION	1943
DATE SUNK	Unknown
CAUSE OF SINKING	Unknown
LOCATION	Gizo Island, Solomon Islands
DISTANCE FROM SHORE	324 ft / 100 m
MINIMUM DEPTH	43 ft / 13 m
MAXIMUM DEPTH	49 ft / 15 m
LENGTH	32 ft / 10 m

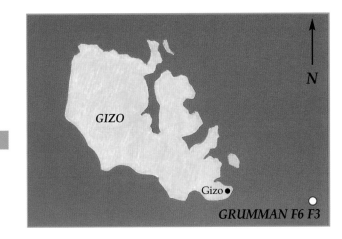

GIZO

N

Gizo ●

GRUMMAN F6 F3

During the first phase of the war in the Pacific, the Allies struggled to combat Japanese fighters, especially the legendary Zeros. While the Grumman F4 F3 Wildcat was more powerful and better armed, it was much less agile and manageable, and thus often succumbed in direct combat.

It was not until 1943, when the Grumman F6 F3 Hellcat came into service, that the balance clearly shifted in favor of the Americans, who also had the excellent Chance Vought F4U Corsair.

The Hellcat was a versitile war machine, and when it joined the US Navy it garnered over 6000 victories, significantly contributing to the destruction of Japanese air power. There is no accurate information on the history of the plane that crashed near Gizo Island, located in the immediate vicinity of the island on

226 top and 227 top The Hellcat engaged in vicious duels with the Zeros during World War II.

227 center left The plane carried a Pratt & Whitney 2800 CV engine giving it a speed of 375 mph (605 kmh).

227 center right The Hellcat was a 33 ft (10 m) long fighter plane. It could fly at an altitude 5,300 and had a range of about 930 miles (1,500 km).

227 bottom left The Hellcat fell near the island of Kennedy and rests on an approximately 50 ft (15 m) coral reef.

43 ft / 13 m

49 ft / 15 m

which John F. Kennedy, future President of the United States, had his own misadventure. In August 1943, during a patrol operation while he was in command of the torpedo boat PT-109, his boat was rammed by the Japanese destroyer the *Amagiri*. The torpedo boat was broken in two by the impact, and while the stern section was dragged to the bottom by the weight of the engines, the bow stayed afloat because of its watertight compartments, listing with the few survivors. They reached the island of Kaslol, still in Japanese hands, and here rescued only after a

week of hiding in the palm groves.

The Hellcat, resting upright on a sandy coral sea floor at a depth of about 49 ft (15 m), is almost fully intact and shows no clear signs of a gunfight. This leads us to believe that a flight emergency is what caused it to make a water landing. The fuselage, tail and left wing are in good condition, while the right wing is broken. The rudder coverings are also completely missing, along with all the propeller blades, which were probably destroyed on impact. The aluminum wreck has not been colonized by much coral,

228 The body, tail, and left wing are in good condition, while the right wing is broken. The surface of the rudders and all the propeller blades are missing; probably destroyed upon impact with the water.

229 top The radial engine that is visible in the forefront has striking dimensions. The exploration of the wreck can begin almost anywhere, depending on preferred perspectives.

229 bottom The housing for ammunition supplied the 6 machine guns onboard, providing 2350 shots. The armament included 5500 lb (2250 kg) bombs, or, alternatively, 6 rockets.

and when the water is clear, the plane is perfectly visible from the surface. Because of its small size, not much time is required to explore the wreck, and you can begin near the surface, following various angles. The powerful radial engine dominates the rest of the plane. Stopping to look at the right wing, you'll see the two deadly 12.7-mm machine guns on the front side. A large number of bullets remain intact in the ammunition magazine on the upper surface of the wing. All the instruments have vanished from the single-seater cockpit, while the control stick and rudder bar remain, still slightly mobile. The open sliding canopy leads us to believe that after the pilot made his water landing, he managed to get out of the plane before it sank and was able to reach the nearby beach.

B-17 E

BY VINCENZO PAOLILLO

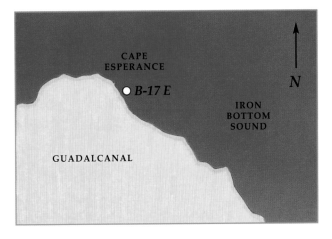

23 ft / 7 m

39 ft / 12 m

CAPE
ESPERANCE

B-17 E

N

IRON
BOTTOM
SOUND

GUADALCANAL

I n the great crucible of the war in the Pacific, fought in inhospitable, often uninhabited areas or regions where the population spoke only their native tongue, it's uncommon to receive information about small, individual, yet dramatic wartime events.

The case of the B-17 E Flying Fortress nicknamed "Bessie Jap Smasher" is an exception. The B-17 was at that time by far the most powerful bomber used in the war in the Pacific; it could carry 17640 lbs (8000 kg) of bombs, had a flying range of about 1860 miles (3,000 km), and flew at a speed of almost 310 mph (500 kph). On August 24, 1942, "Bessie Jap Smasher," part of the 42nd Bombardment Squadron, took off from the recently occupied and repaired airport at Henderson Field (now Honiara International Airport) on Guadalcanal. Chief pilot Lt. Charles E. Norton captained a crew of 8 men taking the formidable bomber on a strike mission against Japanese positions on Shortland Island in the Western Solomons.

Just as Lt. Norton was releasing his cargo of destruction, a Japanese fighter squadron attacked and seriously damaged the aircraft. With one engine out of action and the propeller of another riddled with bullet holes, Norton almost managed to reach his airport on Guadalcanal, only 5 minutes and less than 12.5 miles (20 km) away. But en route he either came under further attack by the Japanese (they were everywhere) or found himself flying against the wind and unable to continue. He had to try a water landing only 324 ft

(100 m) from the beach of Guadalcanal. The maneuver was unsuccessful and the airplane sank. The entire crew supposedly escaped alive, but what became of them no one knows. Perhaps the wounded men drowned, or perhaps the attacking Zeros continued to fire, killing them as they were trying to reach the beach.

All that is certain is that the body of machine-gunner Sgt. Bruce Osborne was found some time later on the beach, and that after 6 days of wandering, the captain was captured by the Japanese troops who still occupied that zone. According to official documents, he died upon arrival at Japanese headquarters.

A year and a half later, when Guadalcanal was firmly in American hands, attempts were made to recover the bomber: the only result was verification that there were no bodies inside and that the plane had shifted position, now facing the sea instead of the shore.

The dive is very simple. Just jump in from the pebble beach, and a little farther, at a depth of 23 ft (7 m), where the sand begins, you'll find a turret detached from the fuselage lying on the seabed, with the barrels

230 top A squadron of B-17s, nicknamed Flying Fortresses, is shown during a mission. In the distance we can see the trail of vapor from the fighters that accompanied them. During World War II, the United States used the B-17 in both Europe and the Pacific: its range and bomb-carrying capacity allowed it to carry out extremely strategic missions.

TECHNICAL CARD

TYPE OF WRECK	Bomber
NATIONALITY	US
YEAR OF CONSTRUCTION	1942
DATE SUNK	August 24, 1942
CAUSE OF SINKING	Air strike
LOCATION	Guadalcanal, Solomon Islands
DISTANCE FROM SHORE	About 324 ft / 50 m
MINIMUM DEPTH	23 ft / 7 m
MAXIMUM DEPTH	39 ft / 12 m
LENGTH	75 ft / 23 m

232-233
The gigantic right wing of the B-17 has large hard coral encrustations. The wreck, which is still in good condition, faces the open sea.

232 bottom left Illuminated by the photographer's light, clouds of fish swim around the fuselage, which appears to be in relatively good condition, at least in terms of its structural parts.

232 bottom right Schools of fish are common throughout the interior of the B-17 they have chosen as their home.

233 top A school of snappers swims around the left wing. This area is very luminous, as the wreck lies in shallow waters.

233 center The diver illuminates a portion of the bridge and flight controls. Farther on is one of the B-17's 13 gun turrets.

233 bottom The outside left engine, which lost its propeller blades at the time of impact, is now home to many young fish.

of the two light guns pointing skyward.

Right behind it is what remains of the fuselage, with another splendid turret covered by incredible red, encrusting sponges and adorned by yellow crinoids.

Curiously, yellow, red and silver are the recurring colors throughout the wreck. You'll see red sponges, crinoids, and yellow-edged lyretails *(Variola louti)*, as well as yellow crinoids, chandelier sponges, and many fish such as snappers, sweetlips, silvery glassfish and splendid mangrove jacks *(Lutjanus argentimaculatus)*. Inside the fuselage is an explosion of glassfish that parts only for the occasional grouper or magnificent emperor angelfish

A little farther, the cockpit has lost its dome, but the pilot and co-pilot's seats are clearly visible, along with the commands, which are sometimes hidden by clouds of fish. Especially splendid is the nose section: an incredible quantity and variety of fish swim below the wings, and nests teeming with life have been created inside the engines. They include groupers, many kinds of jacks (such as *Lutjianus rivulatus, Lutjianus vitta* and schools of *Lutjianus lutjianus*), sweetlips, young batfish, angelfish, and soldierfish.

This is certainly one of the most populated wrecks in the area.

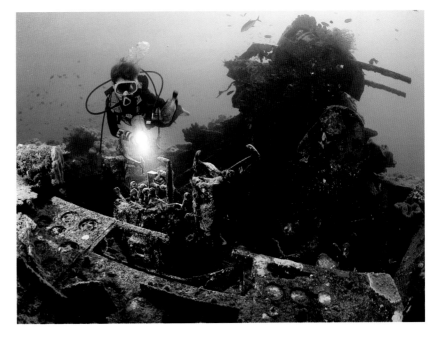

AUSTRALIA

BY ROBERTO RINALDI

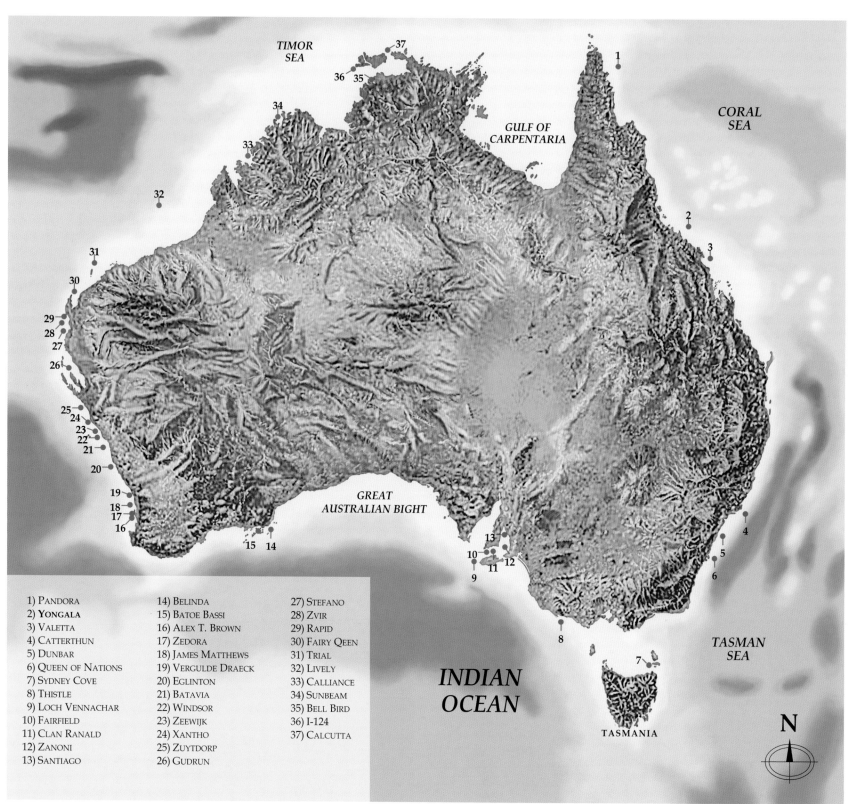

TIMOR SEA

CORAL SEA

GULF OF CARPENTARIA

GREAT AUSTRALIAN BIGHT

INDIAN OCEAN

TASMAN SEA

TASMANIA

N

1) PANDORA
2) **YONGALA**
3) VALETTA
4) CATTERTHUN
5) DUNBAR
6) QUEEN OF NATIONS
7) SYDNEY COVE
8) THISTLE
9) LOCH VENNACHAR
10) FAIRFIELD
11) CLAN RANALD
12) ZANONI
13) SANTIAGO
14) BELINDA
15) BATOE BASSI
16) ALEX T. BROWN
17) ZEDORA
18) JAMES MATTHEWS
19) VERGULDE DRAECK
20) EGLINTON
21) BATAVIA
22) WINDSOR
23) ZEEWIJK
24) XANTHO
25) ZUYTDORP
26) GUDRUN
27) STEFANO
28) ZVIR
29) RAPID
30) FAIRY QEEN
31) TRIAL
32) LIVELY
33) CALLIANCE
34) SUNBEAM
35) BELL BIRD
36) I-124
37) CALCUTTA

234 top Dense
schools of fish reside
in the Yongala, a
vessel sunk in the
early 20th century
off Queensland. This
photo was taken
beneath the starboard
lifeboat davits.

235 top The wreck
of the Nord lies in
the water of Cape
Pillar, southeastern
Tasmania. The deck
in the aft area is,
full of colors and
incredibly populated
with life forms.

O f all the ships lost in the waters of Australia, scuba divers the world over know and appreciate the *Yongala*, which sank in the waters off Queensland, and the *Nord*, which rests on a sandy seabed at the southeastern tip of the continent, off Cape Pillar, Tasmania.

In an irony of fate, the two ships are the same age. Both sank during the early 20th century. Both vessels have similar dimensions. The elegant forms of the bow and stern are similar in both ships.

Both sank in storms — a typhoon sank the *Yongala*, while a gale and rough seas in the Roaring Forties first damaged the *Nord* and then drove her into the reefs. There is one great difference, however. One wreck lies in a temperate sea, while the other is in a cold one.

One is in a tropical sea with the world's most extensive coral reefs, , while the other rests in waters chilled by Antarctic currents.

This makes an exploration of the two ships even more interesting. And it makes divers want to explore both wrecks within an extremely short time span, so the memory of the previous dive is still strong.

This way, scuba divers will be able to recognize the same elegant lines and same construction techniques in both ships. They'll be able to compare the forms of the capstans and the proportions of the ships themselves. And they'll note with admiration that a cold sea is no less efficient in colonizing, adorning and taking over the structures of the wreck as a coral sea is. Large sponges off Tasmania replace tropical gorgonians and alcyonarians, and colonies of zoantharia and small anemones replace the corals. Swarms of fish surround both wrecks. Turtles are frequent visitors to the *Yongala*, while seals climb up to the bridge of the *Nord*. Two different dives on the remains of two ships that share a dramatic history: two dives that teach us that it's not necessarily true that a coral sea is richer, more beautiful and more colorful than a cold sea.

235 bottom left
A big turtle and a
school of large
carangids cross the
deck of the Yongala.

235 bottom center
The Yongala, a
beautiful ship, is now
covered with corals
and populated by a
profusion of fish.

235 bottom right
The Nord was a
vessel about the same
size as the Yongala,
and like it sank in a
hurricane in the
early 20th century.
This photo shows the
engine room with
various gears,
remains of capstans
and engine parts.

SS YONGALA

BY ROBERTO RINALDI

Not all ships were equipped with radios back in March 1911. So, when the message arrived across the ether that a violent typhoon was moving toward the *Yongala*, no one on board got the information.

On its ninetieth voyage, the *SS Yongala* had left Melbourne nine days earlier and was headed for Cairns, the last large port on the eastern coast of Australia.

No one on board knew, but as they cast off from the port of Melbourne, the blind fury of a tremendous typhoon was tossing the waters of the Coral Sea and was racing south at 12 miles /20 km an hour.

Who could have known? In those years, the Northern Territories were almost uninhabited, and there were very few whites. It was March and the typhoon season was almost over. The weather was splendid in Brisbane when the *SS Yongala* stopped at the port. And Captain William Knight paid little attention to rumors that some ships had encountered strong winds and rough seas: all that was happening

north of Cairns, his last northern destination. So on March 23, the *SS Yongala* left the port of Mackay. It was around noon and the weather was still fine. The problems started later, when the ship reached the waters off the Whitsunday Islands — by that time the ship was in a tempest of wind and rain. The sea was not yet too rough, and the ship was still in the lee of the islands.

But past Hayman Island the sea began to get rougher and rougher. Perhaps the captain could have sought shelter at Gloucester Island, but this he did not do. He continued on toward the eye of the hurricane.

The ship finally reached its fatal destination, Cape Bowling Green. She was scheduled to arrive in Townsville on the morning of March 24, but she never appeared. Of course, everyone hoped that the captain had sought shelter near an island or that the merchant ship had only been damaged by the typhoon. And the first rescue boats took off.

The ship was not given up for lost until March 29, when the headlines of the *Sydney Morning Herald* announced that "Four days after its failure to arrive, part of the cargo carried by the *Yongala* was found washed up

236 top right
A painting from the time shows the Yongala at sea.

236 center right
A picture of the Yongala's large stern. From this angle, it is easy to see how the ship lies resting on one side.

236 bottom left
The Yongala's name is seen on the bow and can still be discerned through the encrustations of coral.

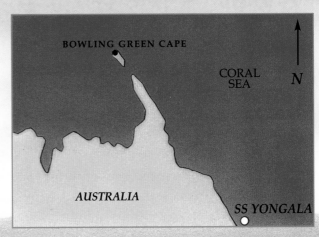

BOWLING GREEN CAPE

CORAL SEA

N

AUSTRALIA

SS YONGALA

59 ft / 18 m

98 ft / 30 m

238-239 Innumerable fish find refuge under the bow of the Yongala's wreckage from the current that is often very strong in these waters.

238 top Numerous corals, gorgonian coral and alcyonarian coral entirely cover the shipwreck.

239 top Many harmless serpents live in the shipwreck.

239 center left In the stern area inside the ship there are a great number of crates with bottles. Unfortunately a law passed a few years ago forbids entrance to the shipwreck.

239 center right A short way from the ship, a large porthole that still has its pane intact lies on the sandy bottom.

239 bottom
The ship lies on her
left side. In the
picture, the
starboard corridors
can be recognized
with strips of wood
from the deck still
on site.

SS YONGALA

along the coast. No trace of passengers or crew. All hope lost." And with that front page story the curtain went down on the history of the lost ship. The *Yongala* was not discovered until the 1970s, when some scuba divers happened upon her, thus beginning her new life.

The fine merchant ship now lies

on a sea floor about 98 ft / 30 m deep off Cape Bowling Green, on the eastern coast of Australia south of Townsville within the Great Barrier Reef.

Today, the *Yongala* is certainly one of the most beautiful wrecks in the world accessible to scuba divers. The ship has beautiful, elegant lines and the wreck is in relatively good condition.

The wreckage has been colonized by luxuriant coral life, including gorgonians, alcyonarians, sponges, and branches of black coral.

The *Yongala* is an oasis in the middle of that desert of sand on which she lies. This is why so many fish swarm around her. When you dive on this ship, you'll descend among dense schools of jacks, trevallies and batfish. You'll be able to admire gigantic groupers hovering motionless in the shelter of the stern or the bow, and see schools of sea bream and tropical umbrines below the lifeboat davits, their snouts turned to the current.

Large stingrays glide over the sand around the ship, along with sharks of every type. Giant turtles rest here. And it's not uncommon to see gigantic eagle rays.

Sea serpents are abundant among the wreckage, with more here than anywhere else in the Coral Sea. The *Yongala* is considered an Australian national monument, so it is absolutely prohibited to touch or remove anything.

A few years ago, it was also forbidden to enter the ship, as the bubbles were causing damage to the structures.

So now, to explore the interior of one of the most beautiful wrecks in the world, the only thing you can do is bring a powerful flashlight and shine it into one of the numerous openings.

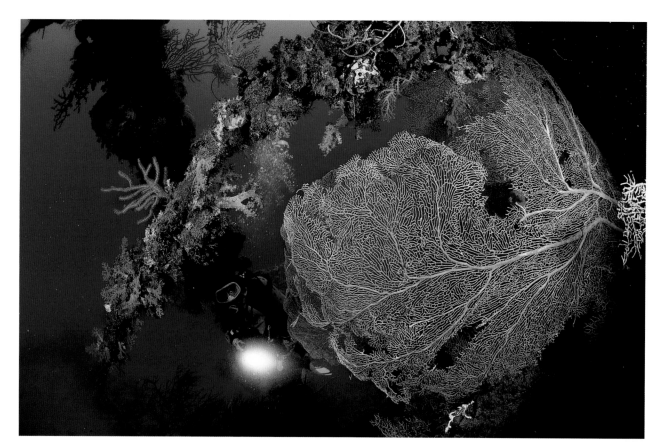

240 A gigantic gorgonian has found its ideal habitat on the wreckage of the Italy Maru, one of the Japanese ships sunk off Rabaul.

PHOTO CREDITS

K. Amsler: pages 14, 16 bottom left, 18-19, 60 top left, 60 top right, 60 bottom, 62 left, 62 top right, 63 top left, 63 top center, 63 top, 63 bottom right, 66, 66-67, 67 top, 67 center, 67 bottom, 68, 70 left, 71 top right, 71 bottom left, 74, 75 left, 75 right, 75 bottom right, 76 top left, 76 bottom right, 77 top left, 77 top right, 76-77, 99 bottom right, 101, 100-101 bottom, 120-121, 122, 124 top left, 124 bottom right, 125 top left, 125 bottom left, 125 bottom right, 126-127, 132, 133 top, 133 center, 134 top left, 138 top right, 138 bottom, 141 top, 141 center left, 141 center right, 146 top left, 148, 149 top left, 149 center left, 149 top right, 149 bottom left, 149 bottom right - **Apostolo:** page 216 center - **Courtesy of Ass. Marinara Aldebaran:** pages 162, 171 top left - **F. Banfi:** page 218 bottom, 218-219 - **M. Bertinetti/Archivio White Star:** page 146 top right - **M. Bicciato:** pages 130, 134 bottom left, 150 bottom left, 150 top right, 150 bottom right, 152-153, 153 top left, 153 top right, 153 bottom, 154 top right, 154 bottom, 156 top left, 156-157, 157 top right, 157 bottom right, 160 top, 165 center left, 165 top right - **C. Cangini:** pages 1, 134 bottom right, 138 top left, 174 top left, 174 bottom left, 175 left, 176, 177 top left, 177 top center, 177 top right, 177 center, 177 bottom left, 177 bottom right - **Corbis/Grazia Neri:** page 65 bottom right - **G.F. D'Amato:** page 215 top right - **T. Easop:** pages 50 center, 51 top right, 53 top, 53 center, 53 bottom, 55 left, 55 right - **P. Fossati:** page 157 top left, 157 bottom left - **S. Frink:** pages 5 top, 22-23, 22 bottom left, 22 bottom right, 23 top, 23 bottom left, 23 bottom right, 24 top, 24 bottom, 26-27, 26 top, 26 bottom left, 26 bottom right, 27 top right, 27 bottom right, 29 top, 30 left, 30 right, 31 top left, 31 top right, 31 center, 31 bottom left, 32 top left, 32 bottom right, 34-35, 34 bottom left, 35 top left, 35 bottom right, 38-39, 39 center - **S. Frink/Waterhouse:** pages 29 bottom - **B. Harrigan:** pages 36 bottom left, 39 top, 39 left - **Imperial War Museum, London:**

page 231 - **J.P. Joncheray:** pages 72, 73 top, 73 center - **M. Lovati:** page 79 right - **National Maritime Museum Greenwich:** page 36 top right - **Orkeny Library:** pages 240, 241 - **V. Paolillo:** pages 5 center, 78 top right 80-81, 81 top right, 81 center, 84 top, 84-85, 85 top left, 86 top right, 89 top left, 93, 94, 95, 96 left, 96 right, 97 top left, 97 top center, 97 top right, 97 bottom, 121, 126 top right, 128 top, 128 bottom, 133 bottom left, 133 bottom right, 134-135, 140, 142, 143, 144 top left, 144 top right, 144 bottom left, 144 bottom right, 145, 144-145, 164-165, 165 top left, 166 center right, 166-167, 168 top, 168 bottom left, 169 top left, 169 bottom right, 180-181, 183 center, 183 bottom, 188-189, 189 top left, 190 top right, 190 top left, 190 center left, 190 bottom left, 192 bottom left, 192 bottom right, 194 bottom, 199, 200 top, 203 top left, 203 bottom left, 204 top, 206 right, 206-207, 207 top, 209 top left, 210, 212 bottom, 214-215, 214 bottom, 215 top left, 215 center right, 215 bottom, 218 top left, 218 top right, 221, 225 top left, 227 bottom left, 228, 229 bottom left, 229 bottom right, 232 bottom left, 232 bottom right, 233 top - **A. Paone:** pages 80 top, 82 top, 85 top right, 85 center right, 85 bottom right - **A. Rastelli:** pages 52 top right, 65 top right, 73 bottom, 90 top right, 102 top, 106 bottom, 114 bottom, 170, 212 top - **R. Rinaldi:** pages 5 bottom, 7, 16 top right, 18 bottom left, 18 bottom right, 19 top right, 19 center, 19 bottom left, 82 center, 82 bottom, 83 top left, 83 top right, 100 top, 100 bottom, 114 top, 116 top left, 116 bottom left, 116-117, 117 left, 117 top right, 117 bottom right, 124 top, 126 top left, 126 center, 126 bottom right, 127, 128 center, 129, 128-129, 131, 135, 139, 141 bottom, 158 top right, 158 bottom, 160 center, 160 bottom, 161 top, 160-161, 165 bottom left, 166 bottom, 168 bottom right, 184 bottom left, 184 bottom right, 185 top left, 185 center right, 185 bottom right, 185 bottom left, 189 top right, 197 top left, 197 bottom left, 197 right, 198 top right, 201 top, 201 bottom

left, 201 bottom right, 202-203, 203 center right, 203 bottom right, 204 bottom, 206 bottom, 209 top right, 234 top, 235 top, 235 bottom left, 235 center bottom, 235 bottom right, 236 top right, 236 center right, 236 bottom left, 238 top, 238-239, 239 top, 239 center left, 239 center right, 239 bottom - **C. Tait:** pages 45 bottom,46 top left, 46 center left, 46 bottom left, 46 right, 47 top, 50 top right, 50 bottom, 54 bottom, 65 top left - **E. Trainito:** pages 15, 40 top right, 40 bottom, 42, 43 top left, 43 top center, 43 top right, 43 left, 43 bottom right, 106 top, 108 top, 108 center, 109 top left, 109 top right, 166 center left, 167 top left, 172-173, 173 top left, 173 center left, 173 right, 173 bottom left - **A. Vanzo:** pages 2-3, 4, 8-9, 58, 59, 69 top left, 69 bottom right, 70-71, 70 bottom right, 81 top left, 81 bottom, 82-83, 86 bottom left, 88, 89 top right, 89 bottom, 90 bottom left, 92 top left, 92 bottom left, 92 bottom right, 102 bottom, 104-105 top, 104 bottom, 105 top left, 105 top right, 105 center, 105 bottom, 108 bottom, 108-109, 110, 111, 112 top, 112 bottom left, 112 bottom right, 113 top, 112-113, 165 bottom right, 166 top, 169 top right, 169 bottom left, 181, 182, 183 top, 184 top, 185 top right, 186 top, 187, 189 bottom, 192 top, 193, 192-193, 194 top right, 196, 198 left, 200 bottom, 203 top right, 206 left, 208-209, 209 center left, 209 bottom, 211, 216 bottom, 222 top, 222 bottom, 224, 225 top right, 225 bottom left, 225 bottom right, 227 top left, 229 top, 232-233, 233 center, 233 bottom, 240 - **Roger Viollet/Contrasto:** pages 99 top right, 227 top right - **P. Rossetti:** page 123 - **W.& R. Brown:** pages 39 bottom, 216 top - **L. Wood:** pages 20 top right, 20 top left, 20 bottom, 45 top, 47 center, 47 bottom, 48-49, 48 top, 49 top, 49 left, 49 bottom right, 52 bottom left, 136, 137.

All the maps in the volume are by **Angelo Colombo/Archivio White Star** and the drawings by **Claudio Nazzaro/Archivio White Star.**